MONOGRAPHS OF THE
SOCIETY FOR RESEARCH IN
CHILD DEVELOPMENT

SERIAL NO. 212, VOL. 51, NO. 1

DEVELOPMENT OF KNOWLEDGE ABOUT THE APPEARANCE-REALITY DISTINCTION

JOHN H. FLAVELL
FRANCES L. GREEN
ELEANOR R. FLAVELL

STANFORD UNIVERSITY

WITH COMMENTARIES BY
MALCOLM W. WATSON
JOSEPH C. CAMPIONE

MONOGRAPHS OF THE SOCIETY FOR RESEARCH IN CHILD
DEVELOPMENT, SERIAL NO. 212, VOL. 51, NO. 1

CONTENTS

ABSTRACT

FLAVELL, JOHN H.; GREEN, FRANCES L.; and FLAVELL, ELEANOR R. Development of Knowledge about the Appearance-Reality Distinction. With Commentaries by MALCOLM W. WATSON and JOSEPH C. CAMPIONE. *Monographs of the Society for Research in Child Development*, 1986, **51**(1, Serial No. 212).

7 studies of the acquisition of knowledge about the appearance-reality distinction suggest the following course of development. Many 3-year-olds seem to possess little or no understanding of the distinction. They fail the simplest Appearance-Reality (AR) tasks and are unresponsive to efforts to teach them the distinction. Skill in solving simple AR tasks is highly correlated with skill in solving simple perceptual Perspective-taking (PT) tasks; this suggests the hypothesis that the ability to represent the selfsame stimulus in two different, seemingly incompatible ways may underlie both skills. Children of 6–7 years have acquired both skills but nevertheless find it very difficult to reflect on and talk about such appearance-reality concepts as "looks like," "really and truly," and "looks different from the way it really and truly is." In contrast, children of 11–12 years, and to an even greater degree college students, possess a substantial body of rich, readily accessible, and explicit knowledge in this area.

I. INTRODUCTION

There are at least three reasons why the acquisition of knowledge about the appearance-reality distinction is an important problem for developmental research.

1. The distinction is ecologically significant. It assumes many forms, arises in many situations, and can have serious consequences for our lives. The relation between appearance and reality figures importantly in everyday perceptual, conceptual, emotional, and social activity—in misperceptions, misexpectations, misunderstandings, false beliefs, deception, play, fantasy, and so forth. It is also a major preoccupation of philosophers, scientists, and other scholars, of artists, politicians, and other public performers, and of the ordinary person who tries to evaluate what they all do and say. It is, in sum, "the distinction which probably provides the intellectual basis for the fundamental epistemological construct common to science, 'folk' philosophy, religion, and myth, of a real world 'underlying' and 'explaining' the phenomenal one" (Braine & Shanks, 1965b, pp. 241–242). For further discussion of its ecological significance, see Flavell, Flavell, and Green (1983) and the final chapter of this *Monograph*.

2. The acquisition of at least some explicit knowledge about the appearance-reality distinction is probably a universal developmental outcome in our species. This knowledge seems so necessary to everyday intellectual and social life that one can hardly imagine a society in which normal people would not acquire it. To cite an example that has actually been researched, a number of investigators have been interested in the child's grasp of the distinction as a possible prerequisite for, and perhaps even mediator of, Piagetian conservations (e.g., Braine & Shanks, 1965a, 1965b; Murray, 1968).

3. Knowledge about the distinction seems to presuppose the explicit knowledge that human beings are sentient, cognizing subjects (cf. Chandler & Boyce, 1982; Selman, 1980) whose mental representations of objects and events can differ—differ both within the same person and between persons. In the within-person case, for example, I may be aware both that something

appears to be A and that it really is B. I could also be aware that it might appear to be C under special viewing conditions or that I pretended or fantasized that it was D yesterday. I may know that these are all possible ways that I can "represent" the very same thing (perceive it, encode it, know it, interpret it, construe it, think about it—although inadequate, the term "represent" will have to do). In the between-persons case, I may be aware that you might represent the same thing differently than I do because our perceptual, conceptual, or affective perspectives on it might differ. If this analysis is correct, knowledge about the appearance-reality distinction is but one instance of our more general knowledge that the selfsame object or event can be "represented" (apprehended, experienced, etc.) in different ways by the same person and by different people. On this analysis, then, its development is worth studying because it is part of the larger development of our conscious knowledge about our own and other minds—thus of metacognition (e.g., Brown, Bransford, Ferrara, & Campione, 1983; Flavell, 1985; Wellman, 1985) and of social cognition (e.g., Flavell, 1985; Shantz, 1983). We return to this line of reasoning in Chapter 9.

The development of early forms of this knowledge in preschool children has been investigated by Braine and Shanks (1965a, 1965b), Daehler (1970), DeVries (1969), Elkind (1966), King (1971), Langer and Strauss (1972), Murray (1965, 1968), Tronick and Hershenson (1979), and, most recently and systematically, Flavell and colleagues (Flavell, Flavell, & Green, 1983; Flavell, Zhang, Zou, Dong, & Qi, 1983; Taylor & Flavell, 1984). A brief report of our work illustrates how this knowledge can be assessed and summarizes what little is presently known about its early development. For a review of some of the earlier work, see Flavell, Flavell, and Green (1983).

Our studies assessed the ability of 3–5-year-olds to distinguish between and correctly identify real versus apparent object properties (color, size, and shape), object identities, object presence-absence, and action identities. Following a brief explanation and demonstration of the meaning of "looks like" and "really and truly," subjects were presented with illusory stimuli—for example, a sponge that looks like a rock or a white object that looks blue when viewed through a blue filter. After discovering what property or object identity the stimuli really possessed (their reality), the children were asked to report both what the stimuli looked like and what they really and truly were. A small minority of even the younger subjects was clearly able to distinguish conceptually between appearance and reality in these simple task situations, and the percentage of subjects who could do so increased significantly between 3 and 5 years of age. However, most of the younger subjects and even some of the older ones did not perform well on these tasks. Moreover, the types of errors the poor performers made showed a fairly systematic pattern. When questioned about object properties, they tended to report that the illusory stimulus not only looked the color, size, or shape it presently appeared to be but also really and truly was that color, size, or shape (a *phenomenism error pattern*). For example, they would say that the white object both looked blue and really was blue. (It really was, of course, but even adults do not know that, unless they have learned how color vision works.) When questioned about object identities, object presence-absence, and action identities, on the other hand, they were likelier to make the opposite error; that is, they often incorrectly reported that the stimulus presently looked like what it really and truly was (an *intellectual realism pattern*). For example, they would say that the imitation rock both looked like a sponge and really was a sponge. One of Flavell's studies of American 3–5-year-olds was replicated with Mandarin-speaking Chinese 3–5-year-olds in the People's Republic of China (Flavell, Zhang, Zou, Dong, & Qi, 1983). The error patterns, age changes, and absolute levels of performance were very similar in the two samples.

The present studies were designed to answer two sets of questions about the development of the appearance-reality distinction. The first concerns the knowledge and skills regarding the distinction that 3-year-olds do and do not possess. Three-year-olds are of special interest because they are the youngest children who can meaningfully be tested on the easiest Appearance-Reality (AR) tasks we have been able to devise thus far. Children of 4 and 5 are of less interest because we have already shown that they can manage these tasks better (Flavell, Flavell, & Green, 1983). The second question deals with developments in this area that occur after early childhood.

1. We have seen that most 3-year-olds perform poorly on simple AR tasks. How should this poor performance be interpreted? Perhaps these tasks are valid and sensitive measures of young children's basic competence in this area, and their poor performance on them simply means that they lack such competence. On the other hand, it is more than possible that the tasks we have been using significantly underestimate 3-year-olds' capabilities. If there is one lesson to be learned from the recent history of the field of cognitive development, it is that the cognitive capabilities of young children are often seriously underestimated by the tasks developmentalists initially think of to assess those capabilities (e.g., Flavell, 1985; Flavell & Markman, 1983, preface; Gelman, 1979). Consider the following possibilities for assessment error in the case of the present tasks. Children of this age may understand perfectly well the concepts *looks like* and *really and truly* and be able to manipulate them intellectually; however, the experimenter's brief pretraining on the intended meaning of the verbal expressions "looks like" and "really and truly" may not suffice to link concepts and expressions correctly in their thinking. The unfamiliar illusory stimuli used in previous AR tasks (e.g., fake rocks, color filters placed in front of objects) could distract, confuse, or even systematically mislead young children who really understood

3

and could manipulate these concepts. For instance, such children might think that a color filter physically—perhaps even permanently—alters the actual surface of an object placed behind it (much as painting the surface would), or they might think that the experimenter is asking about the color of the filter itself rather than about the color of the object behind it. The unfamiliarity of the verbal expressions and task materials may also make for a general information-processing overload that could impair their task performance. So may the structure of the task itself: in a Color AR task, for example, the object's apparent color is perceptually present—and very salient—when the reality question is asked, whereas its real color is not perceptually present and therefore has to be recalled. This task structure may present attentional and mnemonic processing difficulties that could seriously interfere with the expression of the young child's competence. The question, therefore, is whether 3-year-olds really lack this competence or merely appear to lack it when tested under certain task conditions. A possible way to find out is to see how well they perform after being given more and better training and when given AR tasks designed to be easier and more "child friendly" than those previously used. There is also the question of what other, related-looking abilities might precede or accompany the early development of appearance-reality competence. Studies 1–4 address these questions.

2. What develops in this area after early childhood, and approximately when? It seems highly likely that children would continue to acquire knowledge and skill in this area past the point at which they can perform well on the simple AR tasks just described, but there exists no previous evidence as to what this further development might look like. Studies 5–7 address this question.

As is customary in scientific writing, the studies are enumerated and presented in an order dictated by logical and communicative considerations rather than in the exact order in which they were done. In particular, Study 7 was actually done immediately after Study 1 was completed rather than six studies later.

In this study a variety of tasks involving real versus apparent colors and object identities were given to 3-year-old children. The tasks and their purposes were the following.

1. All children were given a Memory pretest in which changes in an object's apparent color were produced by putting a colored filter on top of the object. The children were asked whether the object will look A (its apparent color) or R (its real color) when the filter is removed. If they pass this pretest, we assume they at least know that the filter does not permanently alter the real color of the object (they might or might not believe that it does so temporarily). If they pass it, they also must know that the experimenter is asking about the object's color rather than about the filter's color and must remember (recognition memory) what the object's original color was. Only children who passed the Memory pretest were retained as subjects in the study. We assume that the above knowledge is at least necessary for good performance on Color Appearance-Reality (AR) tasks. The question is whether it is also sufficient for good performance. If it is sufficient, then all the subjects should perform well on the Color AR tasks; if it is not sufficient, they should not all perform well on them.

2. Performance on four standard Color AR tasks was compared to performance on four tasks that were designed to be easier for young children. In one of the easy tasks (Seal), a small part of the object was not covered by the filter; consequently, visible evidence of the object's real color was still available to the child when the appearance and reality questions were asked. In another (Milk), a familiar liquid was made to have an apparent color that it never has in reality (red). In a third (Glasses), the device that changed the object's apparent color was a familiar one (sunglasses rather than a filter); in addition, its effect on the child's color experience (appearance) rather than on the object's surface color (reality) was highlighted by placing it near the child's eyes rather than on the object. In a fourth (Fish), the device was itself an object that possessed its own real color (a color filter cut into the shape of a large fish) distinct from that of the object whose

apparent color it changed (a small white fish that "swam" behind the large one). These tasks look like they should be easier than standard ones for 3-year-olds and therefore might give evidence of appearance-reality competence that the standard ones do not reveal. The question was whether they would actually reveal such nascent competence.

An assessment was also made of two abilities that might be developmentally related to appearance-reality abilities.

3. First, Wellman and Estes (Henry Wellman, personal communication, 1984) found that 3-year-olds were very good at sorting real and fake objects into "real" and "not real" boxes, respectively, but were not as good at reporting the deceptive appearance of fake objects (e.g., saying that a fake orange looks like an orange). In the present study, children's performance was compared on two types of tasks using fake objects: (a) standard Object-Identity (Object) AR tasks and (b) a task in which children had to say whether real and fake objects were "just pretend X's" or "real X's." Wellman and Estes's findings and our own conceptual analyses of this "Real-Pretend" task suggested that it would be easier than the standard task despite superficial similarities between the two. We also wanted to compare the difficulty level of Real-Pretend and AR Color tasks as well as Object tasks. However, pilot work convinced us that expressions like "just pretend blue" would simply make no sense to most 3-year-olds.

4. Second, we compared children's appearance-reality abilities and Level 2 perceptual perspective-taking abilities (Flavell, Everett, Croft, & Flavell, 1981) in the same task situation. The latter entail the understanding that, even though both self and other see the same stimulus, it may present different visual appearances to them because their viewing circumstances differ (e.g., they view it from different sides). In Study 1, children were tested for their awareness that, for example, a white object on the other side of a vertically positioned blue filter, although presently blue looking to them, is really and truly white (appearance-reality ability) and looks white to an experimenter who views it from the opposite, no-filter side (Level 2 perspective-taking ability). The two abilities should have similar knowledge and skill components. In both instances one has to recognize the possibility that the selfsame object can simultaneously be represented in two, seemingly contradictory ways (all blue and all white), inhibit one's own current, perceptually given representation (blue), and infer or otherwise identify the other, correct representation (white in both cases, in the present example). Consequently, we expected that performance on the two components of the task would be positively correlated.

5. Finally, as mentioned previously, 3-year-olds frequently err on standard Color AR tasks, and the error they usually make is to report the object's apparent color when asked to report its real color. It is possible that the repeated juxtaposition of two different questions, one about appearance

and one about reality, confuses them and that they would do much better on such tasks if simply asked what color the object "is." Therefore, prior to any mention of appearances and realities, we asked this single "is" question about the identity of an object that the child had learned was a fake and about the color of an object that the child had seen covered with a colored filter. If the two-question format is the sole cause of poor performance, children should answer both "is" questions correctly. If it is not, and if, as previously found, Color tasks elicit appearance answers and Object tasks elicit reality answers, then children should tend to answer the color "is" question incorrectly and the object-identity "is" question correctly.

METHOD

Subjects

The subjects were 24 nursery school children (16 girls and eight boys) from upper-middle-class families. They ranged in age from 3-3 to 4-0 years, with a mean of 3-8 years. Six other 3-year-olds were excluded from the study because they did not pass the Memory pretest. All subjects were tested individually in a single session by two experimenters.

Procedure

The following four initial procedures were always administered in the order given below.

Color pretest.—The children were pretested for their ability to name, or to point to given the name, all the colors used in this study. All children performed without error.

"Is" tasks.—The experimenter showed the child a red toy car covered by a green filter that made it look black, handed the car to the subject to inspect, put it behind the filter again, and asked, "What color is this car? Is it red or is it black?" After analogous manipulations with a cylindrical eraser with a Lifesaver wrapper around it, the eraser was held about 1.2 m away, and the child was asked, "What is this? Is it candy or is it an eraser?" Order of car and eraser was counterbalanced, and order of choices within questions was randomly determined.

Pretraining on the appearance-reality distinction.—The experimenter first showed the child a Charlie Brown puppet, covered it with a ghost costume, and said, "When you look at this with your eyes right now, it looks like a ghost. It looks like a ghost to your eyes. But it really and truly isn't. It's really and truly Charlie Brown [removes the disguise]. Sometimes things look one way to your eyes [disguise put on again] when they really and truly are a different way [disguise removed]." The experimenter then performed a similar demonstration and explanation for an object property (real and apparent shape) rather than an object identity. The purpose of the pretraining was to try to ensure that children capable of appreciating the distinction would understand which representation—appearance or reality—each question referred to.

Memory pretest.—On each of the three trials, the experimenter slowly slid a colored filter (e.g., green) over a paper cutout of an object (e.g., a white cup) and asked, "When I take this filter [touches filter] off, will the cup look green, as it does now, or will it look white?" The subject then watched as the filter was removed. Order of color choices within the question was randomly determined. The criterion for passing this pretest and thus remaining in the study was two of the three questions correct.

Four groups of tasks followed the above procedures: (*a*) four easy Color AR tasks; (*b*) four Real-Pretend Object tasks; (*c*) eight standard AR tasks, four Color and four Object (given in counterbalanced order); and (*d*) four combined Color AR and Perspective-taking (PT) tasks. Each subject received a different one of the 24 possible orders of administration of the four task groups. Within certain constraints to be noted, each of the possible orders of tasks within each task group was administered to an equal number of subjects; orders of appearance and reality questions and choices within questions were randomized. The name of the object was always used in Color tasks to focus the child's attention on the object and its color rather than on the filter's color.

Easy tasks.—The experimenter introduced these and the other AR tasks by saying, "Now I'm going to ask two different questions about some things. I'm going to ask you about how they look to your eyes right now and about how they really and truly are." If the Seal task came first, she then showed the child a pink paper cutout of a seal, covered all but its tail with a green filter, and said, "Here's the first question. What color is the seal really and truly? Is it really and truly pink or really and truly green? Now here's the second question. When you look at the seal with your eyes right now, does it look pink or does it look green?" The displays for the other three easy tasks were as follows: (*a*) for Milk, the child was shown a glass of milk with a red filter wrapped around it; (*b*) for Glasses, the child viewed a red circle through dark green sunglasses (making the circle look black); and (*c*) for Fish, the experimenter used a string to pull a paper cutout of a small white fish behind a large, transparent blue fish (made of blue filter), saying that the little fish was going to swim behind the big fish.

Real-Pretend tasks.—The stimuli were two familiar real objects (coffee mug, table knife) and two realistic-looking fake objects made of soft plastic (cucumber, melting ice cream bar). Order of presentation was fully counterbalanced within the constraint that fake and real objects were always presented in alternation. For each object the experimenter said, "Here's something," handed it to the child to feel and look at, took it back, and said, "Right now this looks like [for instance] a cucumber. Is it just a pretend cucumber or is it a real cucumber?"

Standard Color and Object tasks.—The procedure for the four standard Color tasks was the same as that for the easy tasks; the stimuli were paper cutouts of familiar objects slid beneath color filters. The procedure for the four standard Object tasks was the same as that for the Real-Pretend tasks except that appearance and reality questions were asked. To illustrate, the experimenter showed the child an eraser that looked exactly like a slice of banana, erased a pencil mark with it, handed it to the child to feel, held it about 1 m from the child, and asked reality and appearance questions about "eraser" and "banana." The other three fake objects looked like a rock, a scoop of ice cream, and a lemon but were really a sponge, a piece of hard rubber, and a plastic pencil sharpener, respectively.

Combined Color AR and PT tasks.—Color filters were positioned vertically between the child and the experimenter. On two tasks (Subject Sees Reality) the filter was positioned between the experimenter and the paper cutout of the object so that the experimenter saw the apparent color and the child saw the object's real color; on the other two tasks (Subject Sees Appearance) the filter was positioned between the child and the object so that the child saw the object's apparent color, as in Color AR tasks. Subject Sees Reality and Subject Sees Appearance tasks were presented in alternation. Each of the four tasks began with a question about the object's apparent color from the child's perspective: "You are sitting over there and looking at that X [points to child's line of sight]. Does that X look Y to your eyes or . . . ?" Two more questions then followed, in systematically varied order. One asked about the object's real color in the usual way; the other asked about its apparent color from the experimenter's perspective in this manner: "I am sitting over here and I'm looking at that X [points to own line of sight]. Does that X look Y to my eyes or . . . ?"

RESULTS AND DISCUSSION

The results are presented and discussed in relation to the five points presented in the introduction.

1. Although all the 24 children retained as subjects passed the Memory pretest, only 10 responded correctly (both appearance and reality questions correctly answered) on more than two of the four standard Color tasks, and 10 responded correctly to none of the four. As Table 1 shows, the numbers of subjects responding correctly on each task ranged from 10 to 13 with a mean of 11.5. These results cannot be taken to imply that 3-year-olds always

TABLE 1

NUMBER OF CHILDREN ($N = 24$) RESPONDING
CORRECTLY ON APPEARANCE-REALITY
(AR) AND RELATED TASKS

Task	Correct Responses (N)
Easy AR:	
Seal.....................	19
Milk	11
Glasses	11
Fish.....................	12
Standard AR:[a]	
Color	11.5
	(10–13)
Object...................	11.5
	(11–12)
Real-Pretend[b]...............	18.5
	(18–19)
"Is":	
Color	13
Object...................	23

[a] Data are means and ranges (in parentheses) for four tasks.
[b] Data are means and ranges (in parentheses) for the four possible pairs of real and fake objects.

can or always do maintain the object's original color in focal attention when answering reality questions or that they necessarily represent the object as continuing to possess that color while it is still under the filter. However, they do suggest that being able to (a) realize that the experimenter is talking about the object's color rather than about the filter's color, (b) remember what color the object was before the filter was put over it, and (c) understand that it will look that same color again when the filter is removed is not sufficient to ensure good performance on Color AR tasks. Clearly, young children can possess these three abilities and still perform poorly.

2. As Table 1 also shows, children performed no better on the easy Milk, Glasses, and Fish Color tasks than on their standard counterparts. On the Seal task, eight of the 24 children gave the real color "pink" in response to the appearance question—not unreasonably, given that the seal's pink tail was visible. Seven of these eight subjects also reported that the seal really and truly was pink. We credited these children with correct responses to the task but do not feel confident that they understood the appearance-reality distinction. However, of the remaining 16 children, 12 answered both questions correctly, a 75% success rate. This success rate is somewhat higher than that of the other seemingly easy tasks (range of 46%–50%). Thus, although providing visible evidence of the object's real color (Seal) may have been somewhat helpful, our other attempts to make the Color AR task easier were surprisingly ineffective. It did not facilitate performance at all to make

a highly familiar substance's apparent color one that the child never sees that substance display in everyday life (Milk), or to position a familiar device for changing apparent color next to the child's eyes rather than next to the object's surface (Glasses), or to make the apparent color be the real color of another object that the target object just happens to move behind (Fish).

3. Performance on the Real-Pretend tasks is presented in Table 1 in terms of pairs of Real and Pretend tasks correctly responded to, in order to make it more comparable to performance on the standard Object AR tasks, each of which contained a pair of questions (one about appearance, one about reality); the scores on the four Real-Pretend tasks taken separately are thus higher than what is shown in Table 1 ($M = 21$, range $= 20$–23). In Wellman and Estes's study (Wellman, personal communication, 1984), 92% of subjects' real–not real identifications were correct; in ours, 88% of subjects' real-pretend identifications were correct. Also consistent with their findings, our 3-year-olds tended to perform better on Real-Pretend tasks than on standard Object AR tasks; they answered correctly a higher proportion of the former four questions than of the latter eight questions ($p < .07$ by Sign test). There are several reasons why Real-Pretend tasks might be easier: (a) the child does not have to distinguish between and answer two different questions on these tasks; (b) the child does not have to represent explicitly the object's appearance and differentiate it from its reality but only to indicate what sort of object it is—real (perhaps "normal") versus pretend (perhaps "abnormal")—and (c) *pretend* and *not real* are probably familiar concepts to 3-year-olds from their pretend play and other experiences (e.g., Bretherton, 1984; see also Chap. 10). Whatever the reasons, the Real-Pretend data show that 3-year-olds do possess some knowledge relevant to the appearance-reality distinction and can perform consistently correctly on some tasks in this domain.

4. Not surprisingly, children performed almost perfectly on two parts of the combined Color AR and PT tasks: (a) the four appearance-for-self questions and (b) the two reality questions on the Subject Sees Reality tasks, in which they viewed the real rather than the illusory apparent color. These six questions could be correctly answered simply by reporting the color that was presently visible to the self and are therefore of little interest. Children performed less well, and at about the same level, on the four appearance-for-other (perspective-taking) questions and the two reality questions on the Subject Sees Appearance tasks, in which they viewed the apparent rather than the real color: the numbers of children responding correctly to the former four and the latter two questions were 17, 17, 15, and 15 and 16 and 13, respectively. The 3-year-olds' performance on these four perspective-taking questions is consistent with previous findings using different Level 2 tasks (Flavell, Everett, Croft, & Flavell, 1981). Correlational analyses were performed to find out whether appearance-reality ability and Level 2 per-

TABLE 2

INTERCORRELATIONS AMONG PERSPECTIVE-TAKING (PT), APPEARANCE-REALITY
(AR), AND REAL-PRETEND TASKS

	TASK			
TASK	Easy AR	Standard Color AR	Standard Object AR	Real-Pretend
PT	.73**	.70**	.40*	.10
Easy AR		.73**	.51*	.18
Standard Color AR			.63**	.19
Standard Object AR				.17

NOTE.—$N = 24$.
* $p < .05$.
** $p < .01$.

spective-taking ability might be related. The Pearson product-moment correlation was .87 between performance on the reality questions and the perspective-taking questions of the two Subject Sees Appearance tasks (scored
ranging from 0 to 2 for each question). Recall that on these two tasks the
correct answer to the reality and perspective-taking questions was the same:
the real color, not presently visible to the child. Thus both abilities are
assessed under identical task conditions in these two tasks. The correlation
was .71 between performance on these two reality questions and performance on all four perspective-taking questions (scores ranging from 0 to 4).
Table 2 shows that the correlations between Perspective-taking performance
and performance on Color AR tasks elsewhere in the testing session were
similarly high (.73 and .70)—as high as the correlation between those Color
tasks (.73). These high correlations support the conclusion that Level 2
perceptual perspective-taking abilities and appearance-reality abilities may
in fact share knowledge and skill components, perhaps including those proposed in the introduction to this study. In Study 4 we present additional,
more convincing data in support of this conclusion.

One might also have expected the Real-Pretend scores to correlate at
least moderately with AR scores if it is true that the two skills are developmentally related. Such correlations may have been attenuated by children's
near-ceiling performance on the Real-Pretend tasks.

5. Table 1 shows that on the "Is" task only 13 of the 24 children said the
red car covered by the green filter "is" red, whereas 23 of the 24 said the
eraser that looked like Lifesavers candy "is" an eraser. This pattern is consistent with previous findings that, for children who err, Color tasks tend to
elicit appearance answers and Object tasks tend to elicit reality answers.
More important, it is not consistent with the view that 3-year-olds have a
clear command of the appearance-reality distinction that will reveal itself if
only one asks them a single, familiar question. Children who correctly said

the car "is" red on the "Is" task were likelier than those who did not to answer correctly the reality questions on the easy and standard Color tasks, $t(22) = 1.83, p < .10$.

On the standard Color tasks, children were likelier to respond with the appearance to a reality question (45 occasions) than with the reality to an appearance question (10 occasions). This 45/10 asymmetry accords with the "Is" color result. It is also consistent with findings of phenomenism tendencies on Color tasks in previous studies and in Studies 2 and 4 of this *Monograph* (see Tables 3 and 6 below). On the standard Object tasks, however, they were not much more likely to do the latter (30 occasions) than to do the former (25 occasions). This 30/25 near symmetry does not accord with the "Is" object result or with previous findings of intellectual realism tendencies on Object tasks. However, it is not incongruent with the inconsistent tendencies found for the four Object tasks used in Study 2 (see Table 3 below). For reasons that are not clear, it now seems that AR tasks involving color and other properties elicit phenomenism errors more dependably than tasks involving object identities elicit intellectual realism errors. Perhaps some of the phenomenistic responses to objects are the result of the children spontaneously encoding them as "(fake, strange) A's" rather than "R's." For example, a child might decide that the eraser that looks like a banana "is" a "(fake) banana" rather than an "eraser" and therefore respond "banana" to both appearance and reality questions. Although we would of course like to understand why young children encode only the appearance on one task and only the reality on another, what seems most important is that they give the stimulus only one encoding, representing it as one, undifferentiated "is."

III. STUDY 2

The main purpose of this study was the same as the purpose of the easy Color and standard Color comparison of Study 1: to find out if 3-year-olds will demonstrate appearance-reality competence when tested on tasks designed to be easier for them than the standard ones are. Accordingly, their performance on standard Color and standard Object-Identity (Object) tasks was compared to their performance on three putatively easier types of Object tasks: Disguise, Sound, and Smell. In the Disguise tasks the child was questioned about the real and apparent identity of one of the experimenters when she conspicuously put on a mask disguise (cf. DeVries, 1969, chap. 5). It was expected that children would be more familiar with this appearance-reality discrepancy through Halloween and other experiences than with the unusual discrepancies presented in the standard tasks. In the Sound and Smell tasks, the apparent identity of each object was conveyed by its sound or smell and its real identity by its visual appearance. We thought that appearance and reality might be easier for young children to attend to separately, and keep straight, if the two were presented via different sense modalities. In an attempt to make these two tasks still easier, at the moment the reality question was asked the reality was perceptible but the appearance was not. In a further effort to facilitate task comprehension and performance on these five types of tasks, each was immediately preceded by pretraining on exactly that kind of Appearance-Reality (AR) task. In all previous research in this area, as in common parlance, "appearance" has been synonymous with "visual appearance." A secondary purpose of using the Sound and Smell tasks was to find out how young children respond to illusory auditory and olfactory appearances. Finally, the Study 1 Memory pretest was also administered in this study; in this study, however, children were not excluded from the study if they performed below criterion. We wanted to see if good performance on this pretest, although not sufficient to ensure good performance on standard Color AR tasks (as Study 1 showed), might nevertheless predict it to some extent.

METHOD

Subjects

The subjects were 24 nursery school children (14 girls, 10 boys) from upper-middle-class families. They ranged in age from 3-1 to 3-10 years, with a mean of 3-7 years. As in Study 1, two experimenters participated in the individual testing of each child.

Procedure

The children were first given the Study 1 pretest for color knowledge (all of them passed it) and Memory pretest. The five types of experimental tasks followed: Disguise, Sound, Smell, Color, and Object. Each type contained four tasks. Orders of task types, tasks, appearance and reality questions, and choices within questions were counterbalanced and randomized as in Study 1. Children viewed the stimulus through a cardboard picture frame when answering visual appearance questions to help convey to them the intended meaning of these questions.

Pretraining.—Brief pretraining for each type of task was given just before that series of tasks was administered, in order to make task demands as clear as possible. The pretraining was as comparable across types of tasks as we could make it. Each pretraining period began with a general statement about what the child would be doing: "Now we are going to talk about how some things sound when you listen with your ears right now and about what they really and truly are." An object was shown to the child and its reality thoroughly described and labeled. The appearance (incongruous sound or smell, illusory color, one of the experimenters with a clown mask over her head) was then presented, and the experimenter carefully pointed out the appearance-reality distinction: "Really and truly this/she is an X, but it sounds/smells/looks like a Y. Listen. What does it sound like? That's right, it sounds like an X when you listen with your ears/smell with your nose/look with your eyes. But what am I holding in my hand really and truly? That's right. When you listened with your ears, it sounded like a Y, but really and truly I'm holding an X."

Disguise.—The disguises were full, pull-over-the-head, soft-plastic masks of familiar creatures (clown, lion, bear, and the television characters Miss Piggy and Big Bird). After a brief conversation about dressing up for Halloween in masks and costumes, Experimenter 2 went across the room and repeatedly put on and took off the clown mask (the mask used in pretraining) while Experimenter 1 carefully explained Experimenter 2's real ("Ellie") and apparent ("a clown") identity as described above. All the children were previously acquainted with Experimenter 2, and it was she who had brought them to the experimental room. On each of the four tasks that followed, Experimenter 2 put on the mask, stood still for a few seconds, then moved behind a screen so that only her mask-covered head showed. Experimenter 1 then questioned the child as follows. "When you look at her with your eyes right now, does she look like Ellie or does she look like [for example] a bear?" "Here is a different question. Who is over there really and truly? Is she really and truly Ellie or is she really and truly a bear?"

Sound.—The four test objects were (*a*) a large balloon that sounded like a horn as it deflated, (*b*) a "key" (actually, a birdcall device resembling a key) that sounded like a bird, (*c*) a small (5.5 cm high, 6 cm in diameter) can that sounded like a cow when turned over, and (*d*) a smaller (4 cm high, 3.5 cm in diameter) can that sounded like a baby crying when turned over. After pretraining the experimenter showed a test object (e.g., the smaller can), demonstrated the sound it makes, and said, "What is this thing I am holding in my hand, really and truly? Is it really and truly a can or is it really and truly a baby? Here's a different question. When you listen with your ears right now [crying sound replayed], does it sound like a baby or does it sound like a can?"

Smell.—The four test objects were (*a*) a cloth that smelled like an orange, (*b*) a sock that smelled like peanut butter, (*c*) a wash cloth that smelled like peppermint candy, and (*d*) a sponge that smelled like a lemon. The procedure was identical in all essentials to the Sound one except that the appearance question was, "When you smell this with your nose right now, does it smell like an *X* or does it smell like a *Y*?"

Color and Object.—The procedures for these standard tasks were very similar to those used in Study 1, except for the pretraining.

RESULTS AND DISCUSSION

Each child was given a score (0–4) representing the number of pairs of correct answers (thus correct answers to both the appearance question and the reality question on each task) achieved on the four tasks of each type (Disguise, Sound, Smell, Color, and Object). A 5 (type of task) × 2 (question order—reality question first or appearance question first) ANOVA was then performed on these scores. The only significant finding was a main effect for type of task, $F(4,92) = 3.26$, $p < .02$. Post hoc t test comparisons between the five types showed that Object was significantly harder than each of the other four ($p < .05$), with the other four not differing significantly from one another in difficulty level. The mean scores for Disguise, Sound, Smell, Color, and Object were, respectively, 2.17, 2.42, 2.58, 2.17, and 1.38. These results are largely consistent with those of Study 1 in showing that 3-year-olds do not benefit much from efforts—even quite extreme efforts—to make AR tasks simpler and less demanding. It is true that performance on Disguise, Sound, and Smell was significantly better than performance on Object, a standard object-identity task. On the other hand, it was not significantly better than performance on Color, another standard task. It was also not very good in absolute terms: the mean number of tasks correct was only 2.39 out of four, and the numbers of children correct on more than two of the four Disguise, Sound, and Smell tasks were, respectively, only 11, 11, and 14 out of 24 (the comparable figures for Color and Object were 12 and 6, respectively). The fact that standard Object tasks have not proved to be harder than standard Color tasks in any previous study (Study 1; Flavell, Flavell, & Green, 1983; Flavell, Zhang, Zou, Dong, & Qi, 1983) also makes us less willing to interpret the performance differences between Object tasks and other tasks observed in this study.

It seems surprising that the children performed as poorly as they did on the Disguise, Sound, and Smell tasks. Recall that the four tasks of each type were immediately preceded by a pretraining trial designed to show the children exactly how they should respond to tasks of that type. After the experimenter identified the illusory stimulus's real and apparent identity on that trial, the children were asked to identify them. They usually succeeded (66 correct pairs of answers out of a possible 72), showing that they had at least attended to and could recall what they had just been told. Yet they often had difficulty differentiating real and apparent identities on the tasks that followed. Table 3 presents the patterns of errors they made on these and the other two tasks. The lack of a clear conceptual differentiation between appearance and reality was expressed both by giving reality answers to both questions (intellectual realism error pattern) and by giving appearance answers to both questions (phenomenism error pattern); as in previous studies, incorrect answers to both questions occurred infrequently. It is not

TABLE 3

PATTERNS OF ANSWERS TO APPEARANCE AND REALITY QUESTIONS

	PATTERN OF ANSWERS[a]			
TYPE OF TASK	Correct Answers to Both	Reality Answers to Both (Realism)	Appearance Answers to Both (Phenomenism)	Incorrect Answers to Both
Disguise	52	20	20	4
Sound.....................	58	15	22	1
Smell......................	62	22	10	2
Color......................	52	14	27	3
Object.....................	33	34	21	8

[a] The total of the four cells of each row is 24 subjects per group × 4 tasks per type = 96.

likely that they gave the same answer for both questions because they somehow assumed that the tasks called for consistent responding. Quite the contrary, the pretraining modeled only the giving of different answers to the two questions. Further, during testing, the second question was always introduced by, "Here is a different question." As the table shows, both error patterns occurred in response to the Disguise, Sound, and Smell tasks as well as to Color and Object (Color tended to elicit phenomenism and Object realism, but not very strongly). In addition, the type of error pattern was not related to whether the appearance or the reality question was asked first. The following examples may suggest the surprising, almost incredible nature of the errors the children made on these simple-seeming tasks: five children said that the second experimenter really was Miss Piggy as well as looking like her right now and another five that she looked like Ellie right now as well as really being Ellie; six said that the keylike birdcall device not only sounded like a bird but really was a bird and five that it not only really was a key but also sounded like one; three said the cloth really was an orange in addition to smelling like one and seven (more reasonably?) that it smelled like a cloth in addition to really being one. These latter examples and the data in Table 3 show that young children can have as much difficulty thinking about auditory and olfactory appearances as about visual ones. More generally, embedding an AR task in a familiar Halloween-costume setting and creating an AR task in which appearance and reality are presented via different sense modalities and partly nonsimultaneously do not appreciably reduce the difficulty many 3-year-olds have in conceptually differentiating between the real and the merely apparent.

The group mean score (maximum = 3) on the Memory pretest was 1.83; 18 of the 24 children were correct on the third trial. Table 4 shows the intercorrelations among the Memory pretest and the five AR tasks. Performance on the Memory pretest (involving real and apparent color) did not predict performance on a Color AR task, as we thought it might, or on two noncolor ones (Sound and Smell); it did correlate significantly with two

TABLE 4

INTERCORRELATIONS AMONG TASKS

Task	Disguise	Sound	Smell	Color	Object
Memory	.44**	.15	.01	.16	.51**
Disguise		.18	.21	.66**	.47**
Sound			.44**	.31*	.05
Smell				.33*	.10
Color					.37*

NOTE.—$N = 24$.
* $p < .05$.
** $p < .01$.

other noncolor tasks (Disguise and Object). What, if anything, one should make of these two significant correlations is most uncertain. This is especially true given the fact that the real identity on the Disguise tasks was always the same (the second experimenter, a person whom they knew) and therefore probably posed little if any memory problem; nevertheless, many children had difficulty with these tasks. The Sound and Smell tasks also posed few memory demands but were also not easy for many children. Taken together with those of Study 1, these findings suggest that 3-year-olds do not usually fail AR tasks because they cannot remember what the reality was. The other correlations in Table 4 do not form any coherent pattern that we can discern.

IV. STUDY 3

In Studies 1 and 2 Appearance-Reality (AR) tasks designed to be as easy as possible for 3-year-olds did not prove to be substantially easier for them than those used previously. The purpose of Study 3 was to see if explicit training might bring to light nascent appearance-reality knowledge that these "easy" tasks somehow failed to reveal. Thus the research strategy was to use training as a diagnostic tool (Flavell, 1985, pp. 277–278). If the training proved successful, we could conclude either that the knowledge itself was present but not well enough developed to be accessible for use even on very simple tasks (hence the results of Studies 1 and 2) or that at least the capacities to acquire or assemble the knowledge quickly were present. If the training appeared to be well designed but nevertheless proved unsuccessful, we could conclude that neither the knowledge nor the ability to acquire it easily had yet developed.

In this study 35 preschool children were given pretests consisting of four standard Color and four standard Object-Identity (Object) AR tasks. The 16 children who performed poorly on both sets of tasks (no more than one task correct within a set) were then trained for 5–7 minutes on the meaning of real and apparent color and then given the same eight tasks again as posttests; all testing and training were done in a single session. The Object tasks were included to test for possible transfer-of-training effects.

METHOD

Subjects

The subjects were nine female and seven male nursery school children (mean age = 3-7 years, range = 3-1–4-4 years), mostly from upper-middle-class families. One child had previously served as a subject in Study 1 and another in Study 2. As in Studies 1 and 2, two experimenters participated in the testing and training of each child.

Procedure

All subjects first took the Study 1 pretest for color knowledge (all passed) and then were briefly pretrained on the appearance-reality distinction, using the Charlie Brown–ghost demonstration described in Study 1. Pretesting, training, and posttesting immediately followed this pretraining.

Pretests/posttests.—The four standard Color tasks were those used in Study 1. The two sets of tasks were administered in counterbalanced order in pretest and posttest, four subjects receiving each of the four possible orders.

Training.—The experimenter introduced the child to a white lamb hand puppet and trained the child as follows.

Introduction.—"Really and truly he is a white lamb. What color is his tummy? . . . his arms? . . . his back? That's right. Really and truly he is a white lamb. What color is he really and truly? That's right, really and truly he is a white lamb."

Opaque House.—"He likes to play hiding games. He's going to hide behind this house [opaque]. Can you remember what color he is really and truly? That's right, really and truly he is white [puppet pops up]." If the child erred, the experimenter said, "Actually, really and truly he is white," showed the puppet, and then reasked the question.

Red Window.—"Now he's going to hide his real color. This time he'll pretend to be a different color than he really and truly is. He'll hide behind a red window [made of red filter]. Really and truly he is a white lamb. But what color is he pretending to be right now? That's right/actually, he is pretending to be red right now. Right now he looks red but really and truly he's white [puppet peeks around window, then goes behind it again]."

Opaque Building.—"Now he's going to hide behind the apartment building [opaque]. Can you remember what color this lamb is really and truly? That's right/actually . . ."

Blue Tent.—"Now he will hide behind the blue tent. Really and truly he is a white lamb, but what color does he look right now? That's right/actually, right now he looks blue. This tent makes him look blue right now. But what color is he really and truly? That's right/actually, really and truly he is white [puppet pops up]. He just looks blue right now."

Green Bush.—"Now he's going to hide his real color behind the green bush. What color is he really and truly—is he really and truly green or is he really and truly white? That's right/actually, he is white really and truly. But what color does he look right now—does he look green or does he look white? That's right/actually, he looks green right now, but really and truly he is white. Really and truly he is always white but he can look lots of different colors. This red window makes him look red [demonstrate]. This blue tent makes him look blue [demonstrate]. Why does he look green right now [lamb behind bush]? Because you are looking through the green bush. But really and truly he is white."

Powder Puff.—"Now we'll play some more hiding games. I will hide some things so you can't see what color they are really and truly. Right now you can't see what color this powder puff is really and truly [pink powder puff behind blue filter]. How can you find out what color it is really and truly?" If the child does or says nothing or simply reports the apparent color, the experimenter says, "Can you move this to find out what color it is really and truly?" If the child does not say "pink" spontaneously after removing the filter, he is asked what color it is really and truly and, after answering, is told, "That's right, really and truly the powder puff is pink." Then, while moving the powder puff slowly in and out from behind the blue filter, the experimenter says, "What color is the powder puff really and truly? That's right/actually, really and truly it is pink. It just looks blue right now because of this thing [point to filter]."

Car.—"Now I'm hiding a car [red car behind blue filter]. You find out what color the car is really and truly." If the child does not remove the filter, he or she is prompted to do so, and the car's real color is established, as above. "Now you use this [filter] to hide its real color. What color does the car look right now? That's right/actually, it looks black right now. But what color is it really and truly? That's right/actually, really and truly it is red. It just looks black right now."

RESULTS AND DISCUSSION

Comparison of pretest and posttest performance on Color tasks yielded the following results: from pretest to posttest, one child improved from one to four pairs of questions correct, two from zero to two, and one from zero to one; 10 children achieved the same score (0 or 1) on posttest as on pretest; two children performed worse on posttest (0) than on pretest (1). On Object tasks, two children changed from zero to one pair correct from pretest to posttest, six from one to zero, and eight showed no change. Thus only one child appeared to have profited substantially from the training on real versus apparent color, and even that child showed no transfer to real versus apparent object identity.

The children's performance during training was consistent with these results, as the following examples show. The fact that the puppet was really and truly white had been demonstrated and stated repeatedly by the time the Green Bush reality question was asked. Nevertheless, only six of the 16 children answered that reality question correctly. When then asked how they could find out what color the powder puff behind the blue filter was really and truly (Powder Puff), only one subject (the one who performed perfectly on the Color posttest) suggested removing the filter; 13 of the remaining 15 subjects responded by simply naming the apparent color. Seven did the same on a second trial (Car). Even after "hiding the car's real color" themselves by putting the filter in front of it, seven children persisted in reporting its apparent color when asked the reality question.

As a memory check, eight children who showed the phenomenism error pattern on the last Color posttest were asked what color that test's stimulus would be if the filter were removed; seven named its real color and the eighth named a color other than the apparent one. For instance, one child said a red stimulus placed behind a green filter not only looked black but really and truly was black. Experimenter: "Will it ever be red?" Child: "When you take this off." Experimenter (after taking filter off): "Now is it really and truly red?" Child: "Yes." Experimenter (after putting filter on again): "Is it really and truly red?" Child: "It's black." Also, in this and previous studies children often made comments like, "Now it's green," and, "Blue right now." Even though they may have responded to both questions by naming the presently visible color, these comments suggest that they were aware that the stimulus had just previously looked a different color—and of course the experimenter always mentioned that different color in both her questions. Once again, it appears that inability to remember (recognize) the real color of the stimulus cannot account for the severe and, from present results, relatively intractable difficulties many young children have with AR tasks.

The findings of this study accord with those of three other training studies. Braine and Shanks were unable to train 3-year-olds to distinguish between real and apparent size (1965b) and shape (1965a) by providing corrective feedback on each of a long series of trials. Similarly, Flavell, Everett, Croft, and Flavell (1981) were unsuccessful in training 3-year-olds to solve Level 2 perceptual Perspective-taking (PT) tasks, tasks that appear to share knowledge and skill components with AR tasks (see Studies 1 and 4). These findings present a striking contrast to the results of the scores of studies that have tried to train conservation and other Piagetian concepts (Kuhn, 1984). Many of these studies have at least succeeded in inducing young nonconservers to behave like conservers; what remains controversial is whether that conservation behavior reflects a genuine and substantial increase in understanding. In contrast, the children in the present study and in Braine and Shanks's (1965a, 1965b) studies could not be gotten even to behave like children who understand the appearance-reality distinction. It seems reasonable to conclude, therefore, that they truly did not understand it, even minimally. Whether they would be capable of acquiring this understanding by some other developmental/learning route (e.g., through more extensive training than we or Braine and Shanks provided), either now or when a bit older, is of course a question that the present data cannot answer.

Apropos of this question, we have occasionally retested, after an interval of only a few weeks or months, 3-year-olds who seemed as far from such a capability as any in this study. Some of these children had clearly acquired a good grasp of the distinction between test and retest, effortlessly answering both questions correctly on trial after trial. What intervening cognitive experiences or acquisitions might have been responsible for these dramatic changes remains a mystery.

The high positive correlations obtained in Study 1 between performance on Appearance-Reality (AR) tasks and Level 2 perceptual Perspective-taking (PT) tasks suggest that these two abilities share common knowledge and skill components and may therefore tend to develop concurrently. The purpose of Study 4 was to provide a second, methodologically more adequate test of this theoretically interesting possibility. It was more adequate in the following respects: (a) a larger sample of 3-year-olds was used (40 rather than 24 subjects); (b) appearance-reality and perspective-taking abilities were each assessed with respect to two different properties (color and shape) rather than only one (color); (c) the two abilities were assessed in two different testing sessions 2–7 days apart rather than on the very same trials within a single session; (d) there were five rather than only two tasks of each of the four types (thus five tasks each for Color AR, Color PT, Shape AR, and Shape PT); and (e) subjects were pretrained specifically on each type of task just prior to being given the five tasks of that type, as in Study 2, in order to make the task demands as clear as possible. Half the subjects were given AR tasks in the first testing session and PT tasks in the second, half the reverse. Within each of these subgroups, half received Color tasks before Shape tasks in both sessions, half the reverse. Orders of the appearance-for-self and the reality/appearance-for-other questions were counterbalanced over tasks and subjects. The study was thus designed so that the sequencing and content of each child's 10 first-session and 10 second-session tasks would be identical in every respect except one: whether the non-appearance-for-self question on each task asked for the stimulus's reality or for how the stimulus looked to the experimenter. Because the experimenter was so positioned that she saw the stimulus under nonillusory conditions on all tasks, even the correct answers to these reality and appearance-for-other questions were the same—namely, the stimulus's real shape or color.

METHOD

Subjects

The subjects were 40 nursery school children (22 girls, 18 boys) from upper-middle-class families. They ranged in age from 3-1 to 4-2 years, with a mean of 3-7 years. Four of them had also served as subjects in Study 2. As in Studies 1–3, two experimenters participated in the individual testing of each child.

Procedure

Color and Shape pretests.—Children were first pretested for their ability to name, or point to given the name, all the colors used in the study. Four children were excluded from the sample because they failed this pretest. Following this the experimenter first repeatedly explained and demonstrated the meaning of "straight" versus "bent" lines and then assessed children's understanding of these terms. Eight children were excluded from the sample because they did not show this understanding.

Perspective-taking session.—During this session subjects received five Color PT tasks and five Shape PT tasks, each set of five immediately preceded by brief pretraining. The experimenter sat facing the child across a small table. In the Color PT pretraining the experimenter showed the child a cutout of a pink seal, said, "Here's a pink seal," placed it on the table on her side of a vertical blue filter, and said, "The seal looks blue to you because you're looking through this thing [indicates filter]. I'm looking at the seal too, but it looks pink to me. Now [places seal on the child's side of the filter] the seal looks pink to your eyes but it looks blue to my eyes." In the Shape PT pretraining the experimenter began by reminding the child, with gestures, about the meaning of "bent" and "straight" lines. Then she showed the child an arc-shaped piece of plastic straw, said, "Here's a bent straw," held it behind a small cylindrical bottle of fluid so that it looked straight to the child, and then described, as above, the apparent shape for her versus that for the child when positioned on each side of the bottle ("The straw looks straight to you because . . ."). On the PT tasks the experimenter showed the child the object (but did not name its color or shape), placed it on her side of the illusion-giving device, and said, "Here's an X. Here's the first/ second question. You are looking at the X with your eyes right now. Does it look A [e.g., blue, bent] to you or does it look B to you? Here's the second/ first question. I'm looking at the X with my eyes right now. Does it look A to me or does it look B to me?" The real shapes of the objects used on the Shape PT tasks were straight on Tasks 1, 3, and 5 and bent on Tasks 2 and 4. Bottles of fluid and a folded plastic lens were used to make the bent objects look straight and the straight ones bent from the subject's perspective. Color filters were used to produce changes in apparent color. The five tasks of each type were administered in a fixed order that was the same for all subjects and the same in both testing sessions.

Appearance-Reality session.—Pretraining and testing were the same as in the PT session except that the non-appearance-for-self question always concerned the object's real shape or color ("What color/shape is the X really and truly? Is it really and truly A or is it really and truly B?") rather than its apparent shape or color from the experimenter's perspective. As indicated previously, the answers to the AR reality question and the PT experimenter's-perspective question were always the same for any given task because the object's real color or shape was in fact always visible from her perspective.

RESULTS AND DISCUSSION

Two scores were used in data analyses: (*a*) number of pairs of correct answers to the two questions of each task and (*b*) number of correct answers to the non-appearance-for-self question. We assume that *a* may provide a slightly better index of the child's ability to discriminate between and correctly identify appearance for self and reality (appearance-reality ability) and appearance for self and appearance for other (perspective-taking ability). Table 5 shows the intercorrelations among AR and PT tasks using both measures. For pairs scores, the correlation between Color AR and Color PT is .67, that between Shape AR and Shape PT is .72, and that between total (Color plus Shape) AR and total PT is .75. The other, single-answer scores yielded similar correlations (above the diagonal in Table 5). Recall that the AR and PT task data were obtained in different testing sessions separated by several days and were given in response to different questions. In contrast, the data from the Color and Shape AR tasks were obtained in the same

TABLE 5

INTERCORRELATIONS AMONG APPEARANCE-REALITY (AR) AND
PERSPECTIVE-TAKING (PT) TASKS

	Color AR	Color PT	Shape AR	Shape PT
Color AR	(.87)	.64	.70	.47
Color PT.....................	.67	(.86)	.44	.53
Shape AR.....................	.73	.57	(.71)	.70
Shape PT	.63	.69	.72	(.70)

NOTE.—$N = 40$. The correlations in parentheses are between subjects' performance on Tasks 1, 3, and 4 and their performance on Tasks 2 and 5 and are thus estimates of the test reliability of each type of task. These correlations and those below the diagonal are based on correct answers to both the subject's-appearance question and the reality/experimenter's-appearance question (thus on correct pairs of answers). Those above the diagonal are based on correct answers only to the reality/experimenter's-appearance question. All the correlations in the table are significant ($p < .01$).

TABLE 6

Patterns of Answers to Appearance-for-Self, Reality, and
Appearance-for-Other Questions

	Patterns of Answers[a]			
Type of Task	Correct Answers to Both	Reality or Appearance-for-Other Answers to Both	Appearance-for-Self Answers to Both	Incorrect Answers to Both
Color AR	85	4	103	8
Shape AR	77	29	77	17
Color PT............	107	3	85	5
Shape PT	84	29	68	19

[a] The total of the four cells of each row is 40 subjects × 5 tasks per type = 200.

testing session and were given in response to very similar questions; the same was true for the Color and Shape PT tasks. Nevertheless, the correlations between Color and Shape tasks (for pairs scores, .73 and .69, respectively) were not higher than those between AR and PT tasks. In fact, the AR-PT correlations were not much lower than the reliabilities of the tasks themselves (correlations in parentheses). These data provide strong support for the hypothesis that appearance-reality and Level 2 perceptual perspective-taking abilities share common knowledge and skill components. The support would have been even stronger, of course, if we had also shown that these two abilities correlated much less highly with other, theoretically unrelated cognitive abilities.

Table 6 shows the patterns of the pairs of answers given on each type of task. It is apparent that the most common error pattern was to give the appearance-for-self answer to both questions. This is the pattern that would be expected from previous studies: phenomenism on property AR tasks and egocentrism on Level 2 perceptual PT tasks. An ANOVA performed on correct pairs of answers (Table 6, col. 1) yielded a significant effect for type of task, $F(3,108) = 3.03$, $p < .05$. Subsequent t tests showed that children performed significantly or near significantly better on Color PT tasks than on Color AR, Shape AR, and Shape PT tasks (p values ranged from .02 to .06), with the latter three tasks not differing significantly from one another in difficulty. The same ANOVA performed on correct answers to the reality and experimenter's-appearance questions only (thus disregarding appearance-for-self answers) did not yield a significant effect for type of task, however. Thus there is no clear and consistent evidence that Level 2 perceptual perspective-taking abilities develop earlier than appearance-reality abilities or the reverse. Rather the correlational evidence suggests that some common set of acquired skills and knowledge may help mediate successful performance on both kinds of tasks, causing both to be mastered at about the same point in the child's development.

VI. STUDY 5

The purpose of this study was to explore the further development of appearance-reality knowledge and skills in older children and adults. The study was designed to test the following intuitions about what adults, in contrast to young children, may have come to know and be able to do in this area.

1. Adults possess richly structured appearance-reality and appearance-reality-related knowledge. They have abstract and general schemas for appearances (A's), realities (R's), and possible relations between the two. These schemas make it possible for them to identify as candidate members of the abstract class "A ≠ R" many and diverse instances of appearance-reality discrepancies, including unusual and marginal ones. For example, they might be able to identify a toy car as a possible but nonprototypical member of this class (cf. Austin, 1962). Similarly, they can identify cases of appearance-reality nondiscrepancy (the class "A = R") and can discriminate between instances of A ≠ R and instances of A = R. Moreover, they should be capable of recognizing subtle distinctions among instances of the A ≠ R class. For example, they should be able to recognize that one A is very convincing and therefore, because A ≠ R, very deceptive; that a second is less so; and that a third, like the second, looks nongenuine but, unlike the second, is really genuine. Thus adults should be able to identify and differentiate among realistic-looking nonfakes, realistic-looking fakes ("good fakes"), nonrealistic-looking fakes ("poor fakes"), and fake-looking nonfakes. They could be expected to classify the first as an instance of A = R and the other three as better or poorer instances of A ≠ R.

Adults can recognize that some objects are inherently ambiguous in appearance; they always present two or more possible A's. Conversely, they can understand that a stimulus could be said to have more than one R (e.g., a compound object). They also understand that other objects and object properties are potentially ambiguous in appearance; they may present different A's to the same or different observers, depending on the observers' prior knowledge, previous viewing experience, and present viewing position with respect to them. That is, consistent with the results of Studies 1 and 4 showing that appearance-reality and perspective-taking competencies are closely related psychologically, we expect that adults will often draw on their perspective-taking knowledge when thinking and talking about appearance-reality phenomena. Finally, they know not only how to identify the A's and appearance-reality discrepancies with which they are presented but also how to produce them, change them, and even create new ones. Thus their knowledge about appearance-reality phenomena is generative and creative as well as richly structured.

2. Adults' appearance-reality knowledge is highly accessible knowledge, in two senses. First, it is easily elicited by instructions and task stimuli. Adults should be able to retrieve and apply to stimulus displays their appearance-reality knowledge without extensive training, instruction, or feedback. Instead, brief, fairly vague instructions and a few concrete examples of A ≠ R and A = R should suffice to convey the sort of thinking the experimental situation calls for. Furthermore, as already mentioned in 1, they can flexibly apply this thinking to many different kinds of stimulus situations. Second, their appearance-reality knowledge is readily accessible to consciousness; it is reflective or "metaconceptual" in nature. Consequently, they should be able to describe in detail what they know and think about A's, R's, and A-R relations.

To test these intuitions, first graders, sixth graders, and college students were shown a series of 23 pairs of stimuli. The stimuli differed from one another in degree of appearance-reality discrepancy and in other appearance-reality-relevant ways (see 1 above). The subjects' task was to choose the member(s) of each pair, if any, that exemplified an appearance-reality discrepancy and to justify their choice. The task instructions were purposely made not wholly explicit in order to assess the accessibility of subjects' appearance-reality knowledge (see 2 above); they were, however, supplemented with examples of A = R and A ≠ R stimuli, together with feedback that the latter rather than the former were what should be chosen. We expected that the college students would greatly exceed the first graders in the richness, abstractness, and accessibility of their appearance-reality knowledge. We had no basis for predicting whether the sixth graders would more resemble the first graders or the college students in these respects.

METHOD

Subjects

The subjects were 14 male and 12 female first graders (mean age = 6-11; range = 6-4–8-0), 10 male and 16 female sixth graders (mean age =

12-0, range = 11-4–12-10), and 20 male and six female college students. The child subjects were of largely lower-middle-class backgrounds. Two experimenters participated in the individual testing of each subject.

Materials

Specific materials used are discussed in the description of each task. For most tasks we used objects or created object transformations the appearance of which either did or did not equal the object's reality. Examples are a sponge that looks like a piece of granite (A ≠ R), a blue filter covering a white triangle so that the triangle appears blue (A ≠ R), and an ordinary paper clip (A = R). Among the other stimuli were visual illusions, abstract art, drawings that afforded multiple appearances, an object with an unknown identity, an object with two functions or realities, and an inkblot.

Procedure

Pretraining and pretest.—The subject was shown two pipe cleaners, one straight and one bent. The experimenter asked, "Which one is straight? Which one is bent and crooked?" Following feedback, the experimenter said, "Have you ever noticed that sometimes things can look like one thing and they are really and truly something else? That's the game we are going to play today." Holding on a paper plate a starched piece of cloth about 1.2 m away from the child, the experimenter said, "Now I'll show you what I mean. See this. It looks soft to your eyes. It seems to be easy to bend. It appears to be floppy. It has the look of a piece of cloth that is soft and floppy. [Experimenter hands the cloth to the child.] But feel it. It is really and truly stiff and hard. It truly isn't floppy. It appears to be soft when you look with your eyes but it really and truly is hard. It looks floppy but it really and truly is stiff. Those are the kinds of things we will be looking for in this game— about how things can look to your eyes and what they really and truly are. Let's do some practice." Half the subjects in each group were then given shape training before distance training and half given the reverse order.

In the shape training, the subject was shown a pencil held at a 45° angle, first under normal, nonillusory viewing conditions and then behind a beaker of water so that its shape was distorted. Two questions were asked about the pencil in each of the conditions. The experimenter said, "I'm going to ask you two different kinds of questions about this pencil. I am going to ask you how it looks to your eyes and what it really and truly is. Here is the first question. [The questions and order of choices within were varied unsystematically.] Is this pencil really and truly bent and crooked or is it really and truly straight? Here's the second question. When you look at this pencil with your eyes right now, does it look straight or does it look bent and crooked?"

In the distance training, the experimenter held about 3.3 m from the subject a tiny, pencil-drawn picture of a flower and asked, "Does this sort of look like a circle to your eyes right now?" She then moved to the subject's side and said, "See, it's a flower. Here are all the petals. These are the leaves." A similar set of two questions was asked about the picture, first in the near condition, then at 3.3 m: "Is this little picture really and truly a circle or is it really and truly a flower? When you look at this picture with your eyes right now, does it look like a circle or does it look like a flower?" After the subject had been asked both the distance and the shape questions, the experimenter said, "We have just been playing a game with these things. [The experimenter held the pencil behind the water.] We said this pencil was really and truly straight but that it can look bent and crooked. [The second experimenter then moved 3.3 m away with the little picture.] We said this little picture is really and truly a flower that can look like a circle when [second experimenter's name] stands over there."

Task 1.—All subjects were given Task 1 first. On this task, but no other, corrective feedback was provided. The experimenter said, "Now we'll show you some other things to see which ones would be good for playing this game. I'll show you two things at once and you choose the one that would be best for the game—the game about the way things can look to your eyes and what they really and truly are." Then she simultaneously held up a white coffee mug and a pink eraser that because of its wrapping resembled a pack of Lifesavers candy and said, "Here are two things. This is a mug [the subject was given it to hold] and this is an eraser [the experimenter demonstrated by erasing]." The test questions that follow are basically those that were used for the remaining 22 tasks in the study: "Which one would be better for the game—this one, or this one, or are they both just about as good for the game?" Regarding the chosen object, the subject was asked, "Why would this be better than this for the game?" Regarding the nonchosen object, he or she was asked, "Why wouldn't this be as good?" If the subject indicated that both objects were as good, he or she was asked, "Are they both pretty good for the game or not so good?" and then about each object, "Why would this be pretty good for the game?" or, "Why wouldn't this be good for the game?" Regardless of the accuracy of the subject's responses, he or she was given the following feedback: "Well, actually this one [experimenter holds up eraser] would be better for our game about the way things can look to your eyes and what they really and truly are. This looks to your eyes like Lifesavers and it really and truly is an eraser. This looks to your eyes like a mug and it really and truly is a mug, so it wouldn't be as good for the game."

The remaining 22 tasks (Tasks 2–23) were given in random order with the order of reference to objects or sets of things referred to in the test question varied unsystematically. After the sixth and eleventh tasks the subject was reminded, "Remember the name of the game is how things can look to your eyes and what they really and truly are." The subjects' responses were tape-recorded and subsequently transcribed.

Tasks

Many of the tasks pitted one or another kind of A ≠ R stimulus display against a clear instance of A = R (Tasks 1–15). A subset of these tasks (Tasks 2–7) contained comparison stimuli that had very similar or identical A's but contrasting R's, such as a real piece of chocolate candy versus a magnet (fake object) that closely resembled it (Task 2). Five tasks contrasted an A ≠ R instance with anomalous stimuli designed to elicit thinking about other appearance-reality phenomena, in particular, the possibility of multiple A's or multiple R's (Tasks 15–19). In one task (Task 20), both objects were straightforward instances of A = R. In others (Tasks 21–23), both were instances of A ≠ R but could be compared as to how deceptive they were. The procedures and materials for Tasks 2–23 are described below, together with the choices we judged to be the correct or most correct ones. When the test question was modified, other than to include a plural reference to sets of things, it has been so indicated.

Task 2.—"Here are two things." The subject was shown a real chocolate candy in a brown candy paper and a magnet that looked exactly like a piece of chocolate candy (a bonbon) and was also in a brown candy paper. The experimenter said, "Smell it. Pick it up and look at the bottom. Poke it." A hole had been punched in the real candy so that its white filling showed. The experimenter asked the subject to smell it and look at the bottom. Correct choice: fake chocolate.

Task 3.—"Here are two shapes, a white triangle and a blue square." (Both were made out of construction paper; the blue square was a light blue.) "I'll put this [double-layered blue filter] on the triangle and this [single-layer blue filter] over the square." (The colors of the two shapes now appeared identical.) Correct choice: triangle.

Task 4.—"Here are two perfume bottles." The bottles were identical; the liquids were of slightly different colors. One was dyed water, the other actual cologne. The experimenter opened the fake first and passed it under the subject's nose, giving him or her a chance to "smell" it, and then did the same for the real cologne. Correct choice: bottle containing water.

Task 5.—"Here are two yarn balls. Hold out your finger and I'll let you touch them." The experimenter brushed both lightly against the subject's finger. "Now squeeze them." The red ball was entirely yarn; the green ball had been wrapped around a hard central core. Correct choice: hard ball.

Task 6.—"Here are two white circles. Watch." Using a felt tip pen, the experimenter drew a blue smiling face on one circle and then covered the circle with a clear filter. Saying, "Watch," she then placed over the second white circle a clear filter with a predrawn blue smiling face on it. Correct choice: the second display.

Task 7.—"Here are some blocks. Watch." The experimenter placed a small block on the table and then hid it from the subject's view by placing a larger red block in front of it. "Watch." An identical red block was placed by itself to the side of the two blocks. Correct choice: the hidden-block array.

Task 8.—"Here are some blocks. Watch." A small block was placed on the table and a larger yellow block placed behind it. "Here are some more blocks." A small block was laid down and a larger yellow block placed in front of it, hiding the smaller from the subject's view. Correct choice: the second array.

Task 9.—"Here are two designs." The subject was shown a reprint of a colored Calder abstract design and a paper with curved black lines on it that create the illusion that the center of the paper is raised slightly. Correct choice: illusion.

Task 10.—"Here are two things children play with." A multicolored rubber ball and a highly detailed, authentic looking (including doors that opened) model car were placed on the table. Correct choice: car or neither object.

Task 11.—Holding a white daisy and an antherium (an artificial looking real flower), the experimenter said, "Here are two real flowers. They both grew in the ground and they both need water to stay fresh." Correct choice: antherium.

Task 12.—"Here are two things." A metal spoon and an unusual looking, hard-to-identify blue and white sponge were held about 1.2 m away from the subject. Correct choice: sponge.

Task 13.—The subject was given the experiences of looking through binoculars and then looking through a clear plastic filter at the second experimenter, who stood about 3 m away. Both looking devices were placed on the table. From 3 m away a tiny pencil-drawn picture of a cup was shown, and the subject was asked, "Does this look to your eyes like a spot?" The picture was brought to the subject, and he or she was told, "It's a cup. See the handle. Now I will take the little picture over there again and leave it. Which of these two things [pointing to the binoculars and the filter] would be better for our game when you look at that picture over there? This one, or this one, or would they be just about as good?" Correct choice: filter.

Task 14.—"Look at this." The subject was shown a bottle of cologne that looked like a tennis ball when its green base was not visible. "If we were to use this to play our game, which way would be the best way to hold it? This way [the experimenter hid the green base with her hand], or this way [the entire object is exposed to view], or would both ways be just about as good?" Correct choice: green base hidden.

Task 15.—Holding both objects 4 feet from the subject, the experimenter said, "This is a hammer and a screwdriver. This is a candle." The round, red candle looked like an apple. The compound object had been made by connecting the handles of a screwdriver and a hammer. Correct choice: candle.

Task 16.—"Here are some other things." A rather fake looking plastic fake water faucet that had a suction cup for attachment to a wall was introduced. The experimenter fastened the faucet to the table briefly and then handed it to the subject, saying, "Feel it." Next a pencil-drawn form ("droodle"), shaped like a triangle with an extended base, was shown to the subject. The experimenter said, "This could look like a party hat, an Indian's teepee, a mountain, a sail, whatever." Correct choice: fake faucet.

Task 17.—"Here are two drawings." As the experimenter showed a black-and-white illusion of concentric circles, she waved her hand around the drawing and stated, "This looks like it might be moving." The droodle described in Task 16 was introduced as before. Correct choice: illusion or both with illusion better.

Task 18.—"Here are two sets of pictures." Saying, "Here is one set of pictures," the experimenter showed the identical backs of two colored paper dolls, and then turned them around to demonstrate that one was in fact a nurse and the other a musketeer. The cutouts were placed face down on the table. "Here is another set of pictures." Two photographs of the same man were shown. The pictures differed only in the direction in which the man was looking. Correct choice: the first set.

Task 19.—The subject was first shown a photograph of a picture of a head. Trees and clouds had been drawn on the face. "Here is a picture somebody drew. He drew a picture of a face and he drew a picture of trees." The subject was then shown a blue inkblot. "And look at this. Somebody spilled some ink and it kind of came out looking like a butterfly." The experimenter waved her hand over the contour of the blot. Correct choice: inkblot.

Task 20.—"Here are two things." A penny and a large paper clip were placed on the table in front of the subject. Correct choice: neither object.

Task 21.—"Here are two things." The stimuli were a sponge that looked very much like a rock and the rather fake looking plastic fake water faucet described in Task 16. The faucet was introduced as before. Next the sponge was moved slowly toward the subject, and as the experimenter handed it to him or her she said, "Squeeze it." Correct choice: both or both with sponge better.

Task 22.—"Here are some things." The experimenter handed the subject the magnet that looked exactly like a piece of chocolate candy described in Task 2 and introduced it as before. Next, saying, "Watch," she placed a red triangular block on a white card and then covered the block with a green filter cut to the same shape as the block. The red block appeared black. Correct choice: both or both with fake chocolate better.

Task 23.—Holding two identical green candles that looked like apples about 1.2 m from the subject, the experimenter explained, "They are both candles. This [stemlike wick] is what you light." The candles were turned over to expose their flat bottoms. The second experimenter took one candle about 3 m away, and the experimenter held the other about 60 cm from the subject. The test question was, "Which place would be better to put this for our game? Would it be better to put it here, or would it be better to put it over there, or would both places be just about as good for our game?" Correct choices: both good or both good with 3 m better.

RESULTS AND DISCUSSION

A scoring system consisting of 27 behavior measures was devised to test for the appearance-reality knowledge and skills hypothesized in the introduction. Tables 7–9 contain brief descriptions of these measures. Results for

TABLE 7

MEAN NUMBER OF TASKS (of 23) PER GRADE GROUP SCORED FOR EACH MEASURE

	GRADE		
MEASURE	1	6	College
1. Chooses correct object	10.35	15.65	19.00
2. Correct object and adequate appearance-reality reasoning	2.77	12.73	17.62
3. Correct or incorrect object and adequate appearance-reality reasoning	4.27	17.65	22.27
4. Expresses a contrast or some other relation between A and R	4.81	18.69	22.58
5. Reports an A	7.77	19.73	22.62
6. Makes a general A ≠ R statement	.00	.73	1.88
7. Makes a general A = R statement	.08	1.54	3.04
8. Makes a specific A ≠ R statement	2.69	11.19	11.15
9. Makes a specific A = R statement	1.08	7.27	7.62
10. Understands how our appearance-reality discrepancies were produced	1.65	4.50	6.04
11. Creates new appearance-reality discrepancies	.54	2.50	2.46
12. Talks about own or others' mental processes	1.50	3.96	9.50

NOTE.—The 12 *F*'s(2,75) range from 5.93 to 83.83 and are all significant at $p < .01$. All pairwise grade comparisons are significant at $p < .05$ (Newman Keuls), except that between grades 6 and college on Measures 8, 9, and 11. A = appearance; R = reality.

TABLE 8

Mean Number of Subjects (of 26) per Grade Group Scored at Least Once for Each Measure

	Grade				
Measure	1		6		College
13. Chooses A = R object because it is real and not fake	24	>	12		6
14. Finds fault with A ≠ R objects or other anomalous objects............................	11	>	3		0
15. Reports multiple A's for a single object	6	<	16		21
16. Says object could be interpreted in different ways...	2	<	13	<	20
17. Expresses knowledge that A can change with continued, repeated, or more careful inspection....................................	12	<	22		26
18. Expresses knowledge that A can change with distance from observer	8	<	19		20
19. Says cannot change object's A or create appearance-reality discrepancy	1	<	9		15
20. Refers to expectations or inferences about object based on A............................	4	<	15	<	24
21. Contrasts what is presently seen with what is known to be the case........................	2		7	<	20
22. Indicates that not everything in the display is presently visible.............................	11	<	21		25
23. Talks about what evidence a naive observer would have about the object	1	<	12	<	23
24. Refers to deceptive quality.....................	4		10	<	20
25. Refers to lack of deceptive quality	5		6	<	17
26. Talks about how convincing a particular fake object is.....................................	7	<	16		22
27. Says one object is a better fake than the other ..	1		6	<	15

Note.—All overall χ^2's ($df = 2$) are significant at $p < .05$, except that for Measure 14; values of significant χ^2's range from 14.24 to 37.44. Significant ($p < .05$) differences between adjacent age groups, as assessed by χ^2's ($df = 1$), are marked by < or >. A = appearance; R = reality.

the more frequently occurring behaviors are presented as mean numbers of tasks scored for each measure (Measures 1–12, Table 7) and those for the less frequently occurring ones as numbers of subjects scored at least once for each measure over the entire set of 23 tasks (Measures 13–27, Table 8). Table 9 shows how subjects of different ages performed on each task, as indexed by key measures (Measures 1–4). When discussing Measures 1–4 we shall be referring to Table 7 rather than to Table 9 unless noted otherwise. There is considerable redundancy and nonindependence among measures; for example, a subject obviously could not be scored for Measure 2 (correct object and adequate appearance-reality reasoning) on a given task unless he or she were also scored for Measure 1 (correct object). To assess the reliability of the scoring system, the two experimenters independently

TABLE 9

NUMBER OF SUBJECTS (of 26) PER GRADE GROUP SCORED FOR KEY MEASURES ON EACH TASK

MEASURE AND GRADE	Task 1	2	3	4	5	6	7	8	9	10	11	12
1. Chooses correct object:												
1	20	7	13	11	10	15	14	8	13	15	11	19
6	23	22	16	12	21	17	17	19	16	19	19	20
College	23	25	15	20	25	19	26	26	20	20	21	20
2. Correct object and adequate appearance-reality reasoning:												
1	4	3	4	4	4	3	2	5	0	0	3	7
6	10	21	12	11	19	14	16	18	5	12	17	15
College	20	23	14	16	25	18	26	25	14	18	21	20
3. Correct or incorrect object and adequate appearance-reality reasoning:												
1	4	4	6	3	7	5	5	6	4	3	4	7
6	17	22	21	19	21	20	18	20	18	18	18	21
College	25	24	26	26	26	25	26	26	24	24	26	25
4. Expresses a contrast or some other relation between A and R:												
1	5	5	6	4	7	5	5	7	5	3	5	7
6	18	24	21	21	22	20	19	22	19	21	18	23
College	25	25	26	26	26	25	26	26	26	25	26	26

					TASK						
	13	14	15	16	17	18	19	20	21	22	23
1. Chooses correct object:											
1	2	12	12	13	21	14	14	6	8	3	8
6	13	21	17	9	22	20	16	12	16	17	23
College	18	25	22	22	21	25	12	17	23	22	26
2. Correct object and adequate appearance-reality reasoning:											
1	0	3	3	2	3	4	3	2	4	5	4
6	12	16	12	5	18	15	11	10	15	19	21
College	18	24	24	21	18	18	12	17	23	26	25
3. Correct or incorrect object and adequate appearance-reality reasoning:											
1	0	3	6	5	4	7	5	4	9	5	5
6	15	20	20	20	22	24	19	16	24	22	24
College	19	26	25	24	26	26	26	26	26	26	26
4. Expresses a contrast or some other relation between A and R:											
1	0	5	6	6	4	7	5	6	11	5	6
6	15	20	22	21	24	24	19	19	24	25	24
College	21	26	26	26	26	26	26	26	26	26	26

NOTE.—A = appearance; R = reality.

39

scored all the responses of two randomly selected subjects from each of the three age groups. Interscorer agreement on the 27 measures ranged from 88% to 100%. Disagreements were resolved by discussion, and the remaining protocols were scored by one experimenter.

The data presented in Tables 7, 8, and 9 suggest that our intuitions about what might develop in this area were largely correct. We will first focus on the performance of the college students in relation to that of the younger subjects, especially the first graders. The adult subjects appeared to possess more abstract and general appearance-reality schemas than did the younger subjects. For example, although not significantly more likely than the sixth graders to make concrete, task-specific statements like, "This looks like a rock but really is a sponge" (Measures 8 and 9), the adults were more likely to make abstract, general statements such as, "This doesn't look like what it really is" (Measures 6 and 7). They were also more able to identify, as possible members of the abstract class "A ≠ R," a wide variety of exemplars, including some unusual or borderline cases. As evidence for this claim, they were twice as likely as the first graders, over the set of 23 tasks, to select the object we had decided was correct or "most correct" (Measure 1). They were also four to six times as likely to justify that selection (Measure 2) or another selection (Measure 3) with adequate appearance-reality reasoning or at least to verbalize an appearance-reality relation somewhere in the task (Measure 4; see also Measures 21 and 22). Nonprototypical instances of A ≠ R that they could adequately justify as such included the hard-to-identify blue and white sponge (Task 12), the toy car (Task 10), and the artificial looking antherium (Task 11). They could also identify and describe as such instances of A = R (Measures 7 and 9; Task 20, Measures 1 and 2) and were obviously very adept at distinguishing between instances of A ≠ R and instances of A = R (most measures on most tasks).

As expected also, the adults proved to be sensitive to subtle distinctions within the A ≠ R class. They distinguished between more and less deceptive appearances by referring to the presence or absence of deceptive quality, to how convincing a particular fake object was, and to the fact that one object was a better fake than another (Measures 24, 25, 26, and 27). Even on Task 22, which presented no egregiously poor fake, eight adults and one sixth grader correctly observed that, although both the color transformation and the very realistic looking imitation candy were good for the game, the latter was better.

The adults were more likely than the first graders to say that a particular object (usually the droodle in Tasks 16 and 17) may present more than one appearance (Measure 15) and, more generally, to say how things do or might look (Measure 5). Furthermore, they frequently verbalized an awareness that objects and object properties can present different appearances to the same observer or to different observers, depending on the observer's prior knowledge, previous viewing experience, and present viewing position (Measures 16, 17, 18, and 23), and that these differences can affect the relation between A and R. For example, almost all the adults noticed how the appearance of the imitation tennis ball (Task 14) and the imitation apple (Task 23) differed as a function of how they were displayed to the observer, and they knew what those differences in appearance implied for each object's appearance-reality relation. There is good evidence, therefore, that the adults did draw on their perspective-taking knowledge when thinking and talking about appearance-reality phenomena.

There was also some evidence that they not only knew how to identify the A's and the appearance-reality discrepancies or equivalences with which they were presented but also knew how to produce them, alter them, and create new ones (Measures 10, 11, and 19). This supports our initial conjecture that adults' knowledge about appearance-reality phenomena would be generative and creative as well as richly structured.

The adults' appearance-reality knowledge did prove to be highly accessible in the first-mentioned sense of being readily retrieved by rather vague instructions coupled with a few concrete examples. Recall that corrective feedback was given only on Task 1, after the subjects had made their choices. This might have resulted in most subjects at each age level responding incorrectly to Task 1 and then—because of the explicit feedback— responding correctly to the 22 subsequent tasks. The actual results were quite different, as Table 9 shows (esp. Measures 2–4). The adults (and also the sixth graders, to a lesser extent) obviously had caught on to what our "game" was prior to this feedback and consequently performed well on Task 1—just about as well as they did on the subsequent tasks. The appearance-reality distinction and related knowledge appear to have been very easy to activate in these subjects. In contrast, most of the first graders not only had not caught on to the game before receiving the feedback but also did not catch on in consequence of receiving it.

Finally, the adults' appearance-reality knowledge was likewise very accessible in the second-mentioned sense of being "metaconceptual"—that is, an object of conscious reflection and verbal articulation. They were indeed able to describe in detail what they knew and thought about appearance-reality phenomena, as many of the previously cited measures attest. As additional evidence, they often talked about their own and others' mental processes (Measure 12), sometimes referring to the expectations or inferences an object's appearance would stimulate in an observer (Measure 20).

As Tables 7–9 show, the performance of the first graders was markedly different from that of the adults in virtually all respects. Measure 4 (expresses a contrast or some other relation between A and R) is the most generous and perhaps the best single measure of whether subjects knew what they were supposed to be looking for in these tasks. Only six of the 26 first graders were scored for this measure on more than 13 of the 23 tasks, and none were so scored on all 23. We arbitrarily defined a relatively straightforward and easy task as one on which at least 23 of the 26 adults agreed in their object choices: namely, Tasks 1, 2, 5, 7, 8, 14, 18, 21, and 23. The first graders did not perform significantly better on these tasks than on the others (Table 9). It appears, then, that most of the first graders never clearly grasped the task objectives, even after the quite explicit feedback that followed Task 1 and the learning opportunities afforded by the subsequent tasks. What they usually did instead was to select objects on the basis of various other properties (usefulness, function, color, etc.). One of these properties was the object's reality or authenticity. That is, they sometimes chose the A = R object rather than the A ≠ R one because the former was "real" and the latter was "not real" or "fake" (Measures 13 and 14). Recall from Study 1 that even 3-year-olds find it relatively easy to distinguish "real" objects from "pretend" (Study 1) or "not real" (Henry Wellman, personal communication, 1984).

The performance of the sixth graders was in most important respects more similar to that of the college students than it was to that of the first graders. For example, 23 of the 26 sixth graders expressed an appearance-reality relation (Measure 4) on more than 13 of the 23 tasks, and 12 did so on all 23. Similarly, they were more than four times as likely as the first graders both to choose the correct object and to justify that choice with adequate appearance-reality reasoning (Table 7, Measure 2). They even performed fairly well on Task 1, prior to feedback (Table 9). Thus, like the college students but unlike the first graders, most of the sixth graders apparently understood at least fairly clearly what they were supposed to be looking for in the task displays. However, they tended to be more concrete and task specific than the college students in their discussion of appearance-reality relations. They were also less verbally articulate and, it seemed, less knowledgeable and "metaconceptual" about the whole domain of appearance-reality and appearance-reality-related phenomena. As examples, they talked less than the adults did about mental processes, including interpretations, expectations, and inferences, and about how deceptive or nondeceptive the various stimuli would be to a naive perceiver (Measures 12, 16, 20, 21, 23, 24, 25, and 27).

In summary, the results of this study suggest that adults possess a richly structured, easily accessible body of knowledge about appearance-reality and related phenomena; that children of 11–12 years of age also possess it in fair measure; and that children of 6–7 years of age seem not to possess it. We say "seem" because it is possible that the method used in this study may not have given a complete picture of the younger children's competencies. Studies 6 and 7 were performed to investigate this possibility.

VII. STUDY 6

The purpose of Study 6 was to see if children of 6–7 years of age (first graders) would perform substantially better on Study 5–type problems if the task demands were made more explicit and the information processing requirements were reduced. Two groups of first graders were tested. In Group A, the task demands concerning appearance (A) versus reality (R) were made more explicit by telling subjects that their objective was to "find things that don't look like what they really and truly are"; an attempt was also made to reduce the information-processing requirements by repeating this instruction at the beginning of each task. In Group B, an effort was made to reduce them further by presenting A ≠ R and A = R stimuli one at a time rather than in pairs and by asking of each stimulus a positively rather than negatively worded question, namely, "Is this something that looks the way it really and truly is?" We also tried to find out whether difficulties subjects might have in answering these questions could be attributed in part to the questions' sentence structure (complexity, presence/absence of negatives) rather than their appearance-reality content.

METHOD

Subjects

The subjects in Group A were seven male and six female first graders (mean age = 6-10; range = 6-6–7-5); those in Group B were nine male and four female first graders (mean age = 6-8; range = 6-2–7-3). The subjects were drawn from the same school as those in Study 5 and thus were also mostly of lower-middle-class backgrounds. One experimenter tested all subjects.

Procedure: Group A

The pretraining, testing, and task materials were the same as those in Study 5 except that (a) the task was not described as a "game" (to reduce any possible assimilation to free-play schemas) and (*b*), more important, the subjects were told directly—during pretraining, when given feedback after Task 1, and at the beginning of each subsequent task—that their objective was to try to find things that do not look like what they really and truly are. For example, each new task was introduced as follows: "Remember, we are trying to find things that don't look like what they really and truly are. Here are two things. Which one is better for the kinds of things we are trying to find—this one, or this one, or are they both just about as good for the kinds of things we are trying to find?"

Procedure: Group B

The pretraining was essentially the same as that of Study 5 and Group A, except that examples of A = R as well as of A ≠ R were presented and discussed; this was done to prepare subjects for a series of individually presented test stimuli in which some stimuli would be A = R and some A ≠ R. Task 1 (see Study 5) was broken up into two tasks, one presenting only the candy/eraser (A ≠ R) and the other presenting only the coffee mug (A = R). As in Study 5 and Group A, feedback concerning both objects was given immediately after these two tasks: "Actually, this [eraser] looks to your eyes like Lifesavers but it really and truly is an eraser. It doesn't look the way it really and truly is. This [mug] looks like a mug or a cup and it really and truly is a mug or a cup. It does look the way it really and truly is." These two tasks and the 22 that followed all began with the test question, "Is this [task stimulus] something that looks the way it really and truly is?" If the subject said it was not, he or she was asked, "Why not?" If the subject said it was, no further questions were asked.

Of the 22 subsequent tasks, five presented A = R stimuli, and 17 presented A ≠ R stimuli. The A = R stimuli were the spoon used in Task 12 of Study 5, a screwdriver, a car key, a hammer, and a table knife placed beneath a transparent, colorless filter. The A ≠ R stimuli were the 15 included in Study 5's Tasks 4, 5, 7, 9, 11, 12, 13, 14, 16, 19, 21, 22, and 23 plus two new ones: a Coke can held behind a large lenslike device that made it look small and a curved black pipe cleaner that looked straight when viewed from a particular distance and position. The 22 tasks were presented in random order, as in Study 5 and Group A, but with the constraint that task positions 1, 4, 8, 14, and 21 were reserved for A = R tasks.

At the end of testing the experimenter probed Group B children's relative ability to answer positively worded and negatively worded questions that were structurally similar to the appearance-reality questions presented to Group A and Group B subjects. There were four questions, two of each type. The two questions of each type were presented as a set, with order of type and order of questions within each type counterbalanced across subjects.

Positive question–positive answer.—The experimenter turned on a working portable radio and said, "Is this something that sounds the way it should?"

Positive question–negative answer.—The experimenter tried unsuccessfully to write on a white card with a nonfunctioning ball point pen and said, "Is this something that writes the way it should?"

Negative question–positive answer.—The experimenter tried unsuccessfully to make a nonfunctioning flashlight work and said, "Is this something that doesn't light the way it should?"

Negative question–negative answer.—The experimenter marked with a crayon on a white card and said, "Is this something that doesn't write the way it should?"

RESULTS AND DISCUSSION

Group A responses were scored according to the scoring system used in Study 5. Table 10 shows comparisons between Study 5 and Group A first graders on major measures. None of the comparisons are significant by t test. Recall that the Group A children received more clear and explicit task instructions than the Study 5 children did and in addition heard those instructions repeated at the beginning of each of the 23 tasks. It is striking, then, in view of all this extra help, to find that the Group A subjects performed no better than their Study 5 counterparts did. One might have at least expected their object choices (Measure 1) to benefit from this assistance

TABLE 10

Comparison of Study 5 ($N = 26$) and Group A ($N = 13$) First-Grade Children on
Mean Number of Tasks (of 23) Scored for Selected Measures

	Group	
Measure	Study 5	Group A
1. Chooses correct object..................................	10.35	9.92
2. Correct object and adequate appearance-reality reasoning...	2.77	3.39
3. Correct or incorrect object and adequate appearance-reality reasoning..........................	4.27	5.08
4. Expresses a contrast or some other relation between A and R	4.81	5.85
5. Reports an A...	7.77	10.85
12. Talks about own or others' mental processes	1.50	.39

Note.—A = appearance; R = reality.

because these are expressions of appearance-reality competence that do not require any verbal facility. However, Table 10 shows that this did not happen.

It is uncertain how directly comparable Group A and Group B data are, given the differences in task materials and form of response. If a comparison is made, however, it suggests that the Group B subjects may have performed somewhat better than the Group A subjects, although not very well in absolute terms. Whereas the Group A subjects made the correct object choice on an average of 43% of their 23 tasks (Measure 1, Table 10), the Group B subjects gave the correct yes or no answer on an average of 68% of their 24 tasks, $t(23) = 3.47$, $p < .01$. The Group B children almost always (mean = 91%) correctly indicated that the six A = R objects were things that looked the way they really and truly were. However, they were not significantly better than chance at identifying the 18 A ≠ R objects as things that did not look the way they really and truly were (mean = 60%). Even if we consider only the 13 objects that are most prototypically and indisputably A ≠ R, correct responding reaches a mean of only 66%. Recall that only negative answers to the task question were queried further ("Why not?") in Group B. Subjects responded by describing an appearance-reality contrast (Measure 4) on an average of 4.92 tasks. This means that they explained adequately about half their correct negative answers.

Recall also that, after testing was concluded, Group B subjects were asked positively worded (positive question–positive answer, positive question–negative answer) and negatively worded (negative question–positive answer, negative question–negative answer) questions structurally similar to the Group A and Group B test questions. The numbers of subjects (of 13) who answered them correctly were 13 (positive question–positive answer), 11 (positive question–negative answer), eight (negative question–positive answer), and 12 (negative question–negative answer). Although these data obviously cannot be taken as strong evidence for anything, the children's relatively poor performance on the negative question–positive answer question suggests that difficulties with questions of this form could have contributed somewhat to the Group A subjects' poor task performance. On the other hand, on only two of the 18 Group B A ≠ R tasks did the subjects perform as well as they did on the formally similar positive question–negative answer question—that is, 11 of 13 subjects responding correctly. This finding, together with subjects' good performance on the negative question–negative answer question, suggests that the contribution of the sentence-form variable to explaining children's task performance is modest at best.

The objective of this study was to find out whether children of 6–7 years of age would perform substantially better on the types of appearance-reality (AR) tasks used in Study 5 if the task demands were made more explicit and the information-processing requirements of the tasks lessened. The results for Group B and especially those for Group A showed that clarifying and simplifying the tasks in these ways had surprisingly little beneficial effect on performance. For instance, even when explicitly reminded on every trial that their task was to choose things that do not look like what they really are, Group A subjects performed no better than their Study 5 counterparts. Indeed, the results of Studies 5 and 6 might almost lead one to conclude that children of this age are thoroughly incompetent in this area—that they know little more than the 3-year-olds tested in Studies 1–4, perhaps. Study 7 shows that such a conclusion would be quite wrong.

The purpose of this study was to learn more about what children of 6 or 7 years of age (first graders) have and have not developed in this area. As Studies 1–4 and previous investigations have shown, many 3-year-olds have considerable difficulty with very simple and straightforward Appearance-Reality (AR) and Level 2 perceptual Perspective-taking (PT) tasks. Although first graders obviously find some problems in this area difficult (see Studies 5 and 6), we would expect them to have acquired enough basic knowledge to manage these simple tasks easily. One goal of Study 7 was to test this expectation directly. We administered all the Study 1 tasks except the easy AR and Real-Pretend tasks to a sample of first graders and compared their performance on these tasks to that of the Study 1 3-year-old subjects. Thus the two age groups were compared on "Is," standard Color AR, standard Object-Identity (Object) AR, and combined Color AR and PT (AR-PT) tasks.

A second goal of this study was to find out whether children of this age might possess an even better, more abstract, or "meta"-understanding of simple AR tasks than mere good behavioral performance on these tasks could reveal. We reasoned that asking them to try to administer such tasks, after having had experience taking them and after brief training in administration, would constitute a test of this more advanced understanding. Accordingly, at the end of the testing session the experimenter first demonstrated and explained how to administer a standard Color AR task and then assessed the subject's ability to administer standard Color and—to test for transfer-of-training effects—non-Color AR tasks (Administration tasks).

The final goal was to find out how well children of this age could handle an easier-looking version of the task administered to Group A in Study 6. We were still not satisfied that Study 6 had adequately probed the appearance-reality competencies of this age group. In this version (Choice tasks), the test question was somewhat more direct and explicit, the same property was always at issue for both stimuli within each task (e.g., color), only two properties were at issue over the entire set of tasks (color and object identity), all the tasks involving one property were administered together as a block, and the entire set of tasks was much smaller than that given to Group A (six versus 23 tasks).

Thus the overall objective of this final study was to get a fuller picture of the developmental status of youngsters in the early middle childhood period, in relation both to that of preschoolers and to that of adolescents and adults. We therefore conceived of it as a kind of keystone between Studies 1–4 and Studies 5 and 6.

METHOD

Subjects

The subjects were 16 female and eight male first graders (mean age = 6-8; range = 6-0–7-4). Like the Study 1 3-year-olds but unlike the Study 5 and 6 first and sixth graders, they were largely of upper-middle-class backgrounds. All subjects were tested individually in a single session by two experimenters.

Procedure

As in Study 1, subjects were first given the "Is" tasks and then the brief pretraining on the distinction between appearance (A) and reality (R) using the Charlie Brown–ghost display. Three groups of tasks were then administered in counterbalanced order across subjects: (a) the Study 1 standard Color and Object AR tasks, (b) the Study 1 AR-PT tasks, and (c) the Choice tasks. The testing session then concluded with the Administration tasks.

Choice tasks.—There were six Choice tasks, four involving color and two involving object identity. The four color tasks were always administered first. In each color task, the experimenter first showed the subject two differently colored objects of the same category (e.g., a red pen and a green pen) and then covered each one with a filter. One filter changed the apparent color of the object it covered, and the other did not. In each Object task, the experimenter first showed the subject two different objects, one a fake and one not; the subject then discovered their authenticity/nonauthenticity by manipulating them and by hearing the experimenter describe their function (e.g., "Things stick to this," for a magnet that resembled a cracker; "You can nail with this," for an ordinary, nonfake hammer). The experimenter introduced the six tasks by saying, "Now I'm going to show you two things at a time. When I am finished, one of them will look one way and that is just the way it really and truly is. The other will look one way but it really and truly is a different way." For two of the Color tasks and one of the Object tasks, the experimenter first acquainted the subject with the two stimuli in the manner just described and then asked, "When you look at these _____ with your eyes right now, which one looks just the way it really and truly is?" For the other three tasks the key question was instead, "When you look at these _____ with your eyes right now, which one looks different from the way it really and truly is?" The subjects were then asked to explain their choices: "Why did you choose this one?" "Why didn't you choose this one?" Order of tasks within each category (Color, Object) and type of key question (A ≠ R, A = R wording) associated with each task were counterbalanced across subjects.

Administration tasks.—At the end of the testing session, the experimenter first administered a standard Color AR task and then explained to the subject how to administer it. The subject then attempted to administer, first, two Color AR tasks (Tasks 1 and 2) and, then, one noncolor AR task (Task 3). This cycle of first training on Color AR, then testing on Color AR (Tasks 4 and 5), and, finally, testing for transfer to noncolor AR (Task 6) was then repeated once again. The experimenter introduced these tasks by saying, "I'll ask you two different questions about something. I'll ask about how it looks to your eyes right now and about the way it really and truly is. Here is a _____ [cutout of an object]. Here's the first question. [The experimenter than asked the usual Color appearance and reality questions.] Now you can have a turn to play the same game and ask the two questions. Remember what I just did. I put the filter over this _____ [covers the cutout] and asked about how it looked to your eyes right now and about the way it really and truly was." Two new cutouts were placed in front of the subject. "Here are two sets of things." In turn, each cutout was covered with a different filter and then uncovered. The apparent color of one cutout was conspicuously changed by the filter covering it; the apparent color of the other was not changed. "Which set of things do you want to use to ask the questions?" After the subject has chosen, the experimenter removed the materials that had not been chosen and said, "You set them up." After the subject attempted to do so, she asked, "What two questions do you want to ask?" If the subject supplied only one question, the experimenter prompted by asking, "Is there another question you want to ask?"

One of the noncolor (transfer) Administration tasks dealt with real versus apparent object identity and presented the child with a real object and a fake object (a magnet that resembled a piece of chocolate candy), as in the above-described Choice tasks. The other dealt with real versus apparent size and presented the child with a fork behind a clear filter that did not change its apparent size (A = R) and a spoon behind a filterlike device that made it look considerably smaller than it really was (A ≠ R). Task serial position was appropriately counterbalanced across subjects. That is, each of the two noncolor (transfer) tasks was given equally often in third and sixth position in the testing sequence and each of the four Color tasks was given equally often in first, second, fourth, and fifth serial position.

RESULTS AND DISCUSSION

Table 11 shows performance comparisons between the Study 1 3-year-olds and the present study's 6–7-year-olds on Study 1 tasks. In contrast to the younger children, most (20 of 24) of the older ones said that the red car was red rather than black in response to the question, "What color is this car?" even though the covering filter made it appear black at that moment. As expected, the first graders also showed near ceiling performance on the Color and Object AR tasks and on the Level 2 PT tasks. Clearly, children do acquire additional knowledge in this area between the ages of 3 and 7 years and by the latter age have acquired enough to solve these simple tasks with ease.

Have they also acquired enough knowledge to administer them with ease? The data from the Administration tasks suggest that they have not. Children were scored as having performed completely correctly on an Administration task if they (a) chose the A ≠ R stimulus display rather than the A = R one to ask questions about and then asked both (b) an A question and (c) an R question appropriate to that display. Children virtually always set up correctly whichever display they chose; this variable was therefore ignored. A minimally acceptable A question was of the form, "Does this look X?" A minimally acceptable R question was, "Is this X?" or something similar. Thus the child did not have to add "really and truly" or "to your eyes right now" or present the choice "X or Y?" as the experimenter had always done. Questions produced only in response to the prompt, "Is there another question

TABLE 11

PERFORMANCE OF STUDY 1 PRESCHOOLERS (3 YEARS OLD) AND STUDY 7 FIRST GRADERS (6–7 YEARS OLD) ON SELECTED STUDY 1 TASKS

	TASKS				
	"Is"		Standard AR		AR-PT: Experimenter's View
GROUP	Color	Object	Color	Object	
Preschool..............	13	23	1.92	1.92	2.67
First Grade	20	24	3.83	3.71	3.92

NOTE.—The "Is" task figures are numbers of subjects per group responding correctly (maximum = 24). The other figures are mean numbers of tasks per group that were responded to correctly (maximum = 4). The age differences shown in cols. 3, 4, and 5 are all statistically significant (t test); that shown in col. 1 approaches significance (χ^2 test, $p <$ .10).

you want to ask?" were also scored as correct if otherwise minimally accept-able. The numbers of children who performed completely correctly on zero, one, two, three, four, five, and six tasks according to the above criteria were seven, six, four, four, two, one, and zero, respectively. Only 11 of the 24 children correctly administered as many as two of the six tasks, and only one child succeeded in administering five. This is clearly poor performance, especially given all the potentially helpful experiences the children had had just prior to these color, object-identity, and size Administration tasks. In the case of the color ones, such experiences included four standard Color AR tasks, four AR-PT tasks involving color appearance and reality ques-tions, four Choice tasks involving color, and two separate demonstrations and explanations of how to administer a Color AR task. In the case of the Object task, the experiences included the brief pretraining using the Charlie Brown–ghost display, four standard Object tasks, and two Choice tasks involving object identity. The children had neither been trained for nor experienced previously only the size task, but even it was similar in form to the Choice and Administration color tasks: each of two objects is viewed through a filter; one of the filters changes an apparent property of the object it covers, and·the other does not.

Each Administration task had three components: choosing the A ≠ R display, asking the appearance question, and asking the reality question. The most common response pattern was for the child to get one or two components right but not all three. For example, a child might choose the correct display but then produce either no appearance or reality question or only one—perhaps a reality question that the child might then simply repeat when prompted by the experimenter to ask another question. Or a child might ask one or both questions, but with respect to the A = R display rather than the A ≠ R one. One child asked both questions on both the size and the identity tasks, but the questions concerned the objects' real and apparent *color*—a form of transfer we did not anticipate! The children asked both questions only 42% of the time and asked them with respect to the A ≠ R display only 28% of the time.

Several other trends were evident, none of them statistically significant. The children performed somewhat better after the second demonstration and explanation (Tasks 4–6) than before it (Tasks 1–3), but not a great deal. The fact that most children did not perform very well even on color tasks 4 and 5 supports the conclusion that they lack the more advanced level of appearance-reality metaknowledge that Administration tasks presumably require. Performance on the two transfer tasks was not much poorer than that on the color tasks; surprisingly, the nonnovel object-identity task was at least as difficult for the children as the novel size task. Finally, if a child asked only one of the two questions, it was somewhat likelier to be the reality question. All in all, the Administration task data suggest that 6–7-year-olds

TABLE 12

Comparison of First-Grade Children from Study 6 (Group A) and Study 7 (Choice Tasks) on Mean Proportion of Tasks Scored for Selected Measures

| | Groups | |
| | Study 6: Group A | Study 7: Choice |
Measure		
1. Chooses correct object.................................	.43	.94
4. Expresses a contrast or some other relation between A and R...	.25	.58
5. Reports an A	.47	.39

Note.—The Group A data are those presented in Table 10, expressed as proportions. The data for Group A are for 13 subjects on 23 tasks; those for Choice are for 24 subjects on six tasks. A = appearance; R = reality.

have about as much difficulty in administering simple AR tasks as 3-year-olds have in solving them.

The third objective of Study 7 was to find out how well 6–7-year-olds would perform on what was designed to be an easier, less demanding version of the Study 6 Group A tasks, namely, the Choice tasks. The Choice task responses were scored for Measures 1, 4, and 5 from the scoring system used in Studies 5 and 6. Comparisons between the two groups on these three measures are shown in Table 12. It is apparent that the subjects in the present study performed much better on the Choice tasks than the Study 6 subjects performed on the Group A tasks. Whereas the Study 6 children chose the correct stimulus displays (Measure 1) no more often than would be expected by chance, the Study 7 children made correct choices on 136 of the 144 possible occasions—clearly better than chance, $t(23) = 4.73$, $p < .001$. They also justified their choices by expressing a contrast or equivalence relation between appearance and reality (Measure 4) significantly more often than the Study 6 children did, $t(23) = 3.44$, $p < .01$.

A number of differences between the Study 7 Choice tasks and the Study 6 Group A tasks were described in the introduction to this study. Although it seems likely that some one or some combination of these differences contributed to the Study 7 children's superior performance, there is no way of being sure which were more potent. Differences between the subject samples could even have contributed: the Study 7 children tended to come from higher socioeconomic status families than did the Study 6 children. We believe that the brevity and homogeneity (only one property per task, tasks blocked by properties, and only two properties altogether) of the Choice test may have been particularly helpful to the children. Compare the results for the Group B subjects in Study 6. These subjects had only to indicate whether each stimulus was or was not "something that looks the way it really and truly is," a question as simple, direct, and explicit as the Choice tasks' "Which one looks just like it really and truly is/looks different from the way it really and truly is?" It may therefore have been the greater number and heterogeneity of the Group B tasks that caused the lower proportion of correct responses on these tasks: .68 for the Group B tasks as contrasted with .94 for the Choice tasks, $t(15) = 5.07$, $p < .01$.

In other respects, however, the performance of the Study 7 children on the Choice task was quite similar both to that of the Study 6 children and to their performance on the Administration task. Their ability to justify a correct choice by expressing an appearance-reality relation seemed about the same as that of the Study 6 children: the ratio of Measure 4 to Measure 1 was .25/.43 or .58 for the Study 6 subjects and .58/.94 or .62 for the Study 7 subjects (Table 12). The tendency to report an appearance (use expressions like "looks _____" and "looks like _____") was also rather low in both groups. Similarly, in the Administration tasks the Study 7 children often failed to ask both appearance and reality questions, even after having chosen the correct display.

The results of Studies 5–7 suggest several conclusions about the appearance-reality-related competencies of 6–7-year-olds. Unlike many 3-year-olds, they can consistently report realities when asked for realities and appearances when asked for appearances—whether the appearances be for the self or for another person. That is, simple AR and Level 2 PT tasks no longer present problems for them. This is consistent with a recent finding by Harris, Donnelly, Guz, and Pitt-Watson (1986) that children of this age are capable of understanding the distinction between real and pretend emotion. In contrast their ability to identify on request stimuli presenting discrepancies and nondiscrepancies between appearance and reality is considerably more fragile and task dependent. On some rather easy looking tasks calling for this ability they performed surprisingly poorly (Studies 5 and 6); on others, designed to be easier yet, they performed much better (Study 7). They also find it difficult to talk about appearances, realities, and appearance-reality relations, even briefly and minimally. They often fail to talk about them when asked to justify their correct A = R and A ≠ R identifications or when asked to administer simple AR tasks. They fail to do so even after having been told how and after having heard the experimenter engage in a great deal of such talk. We believe that these difficulties in identifying and labeling appearance-reality relations are at least partly due to genuine difficulties in thinking about these relations as such, abstracted away from the task stimuli that exhibit them. The results of Study 5 suggest that the ability to think about them in this more abstract, metaconceptual way undergoes considerable development during the middle childhood and adolescent years. Thus, although children of 6 or 7 years are considerably more competent in the appearance-reality domain than preschool children are, comparisons with older children and adults show that they still have much to learn.

IX. CONCLUSIONS

The data from these and previous studies suggest some conclusions about the course of conceptual development in this area from early childhood (age 3 years) to adulthood.

EARLY CHILDHOOD

It seems safe to assume that by the age of 3 years or so most children have often had the experience of being deceived by appearances—that is, of at first perceiving something as possessing a certain property or identity and subsequently discovering that it really has a different one. It is therefore hard to imagine that the appearance-reality discrepancies they encounter in these developmental studies would constitute wholly novel experiences for them. In fact, the discrepancies presented in the Study 2 Disguise task were chosen precisely because they ought to be of a type familiar to young children.

Given such experiences, one might think that they would find what we have been calling standard Appearance-Reality (AR) tasks quite easy. To perform well on these tasks they need only consistently select, from the two labels provided them on each task, the appearance (A) label when asked how the stimulus appears to them at that moment and the reality (R) label when asked what it really and truly is or is like. Surprisingly, however, many 3-year-olds seem incapable of doing this; they just seem unable to grasp the distinction at issue. Terms like "incapable" and "unable" may seem too strong in an era acutely sensitive to competence-performance distinctions, false negatives, and the underestimation of preschool children's competencies (Flavell, 1985; Gelman, 1979). Nevertheless, three lines of evidence strongly suggest that many children of this age have simply not yet acquired these capabilities and abilities.

One line of evidence is the very fact that, in study after study, they frequently fail the standard AR tasks. On these tasks the children are pretrained briefly on the meaning of the appearance-reality distinction; the difference between the appearance and the reality questions is emphasized by the experimenter ("two different questions," "the first question," "the second question"), thereby tacitly suggesting that they should receive different answers; and, as just mentioned, the two possible answers to each question are always provided for the children, leaving them only the task of recognizing the correct option. These task features lend credence to our view that young children's failures on the standard tasks are more likely due to insufficient appearance-reality knowledge than to insufficient task sensitivity. The fact that a sample of Mandarin-speaking 3-year-olds from the People's Republic of China also performed at the same low level on translated versions of these tasks (Flavell, Zhang, Zou, Dong, & Qi, 1983) provides additional support for this view.

A second line of evidence is the fact that diverse efforts to create still easier looking, possibly more sensitive tests of underlying appearance-reality competence have mostly failed to reveal any. Of the four so-called easy Color AR tasks of Study 1 (Seal, Milk, Glasses, and Fish), only one (Seal) elicited better performance than standard Color AR tasks. It is true that the subjects in Study 2 performed significantly better on three Object-Identity (Object) tasks (Disguise, Sound, and Smell) designed to be especially easy for young children than on standard Object tasks. However, they did not perform any better on those three tasks than on standard Color tasks, and their level of performance on them was quite low in absolute terms. Furthermore, data from the one-question "Is" task of Study 1 suggest that the two-question format of standard AR tasks cannot explain young children's poor performance on them. Other data from Studies 1, 2, and 3 likewise argue that the memory demands posed by these tasks cannot wholly explain this poor performance either.

The third line of evidence is the failure in Study 3 to engender good performance on standard AR tasks through direct, intensive training. As we argued in discussing the results of that study, the fact that we could not train our sample of 3-year-olds to behave like children who understand the appearance-reality distinction suggests that they truly did not understand it, even minimally. Differently put, they might well have learned to perform correctly without really understanding the distinction, given the nature of the training. That they could not even learn to perform correctly argues strongly that they did not really understand it.

These three lines of evidence suggest, therefore, that many 3-year-olds do actually lack the cognitive competencies needed to comprehend and solve even very simple AR tasks. What might those needed competencies be? Our data are largely silent on this question, but two pieces of evidence suggest a possible answer. One is the fact, observed in all our studies (see Tables 3 and 6; see also our previous studies), that, when young children err on these tasks, they usually do so by giving the same answer—either appearance or reality—to both questions rather than by giving two different answers, both incorrect. They act as if they tend to form only one encoding or representation of the stimulus and then report that representation no matter which question they are asked. The other piece of evidence is the very high positive correlation found in Studies 1 and 4 between appearance-reality skill and level 2 perceptual perspective-taking skill, suggesting that these two skills are developmentally related. With this evidence in mind, consider the cognitive demands of an AR or Level 2 Perspective-taking (PT) task. In reality an object cannot simultaneously be, for instance, both all blue and all white or both a rock and a sponge. However, in solving AR and PT tasks we must attribute such mutually incompatible and contradictory properties and identities to the selfsame object. We resolve the apparent contradiction by identifying one representation of the object with its appearance and the other with its reality (AR) or by locating one representation in the self and the other in another person (PT). But this resolution is possible for us only because we clearly understand that people are subjects who have mental representations of objects and events and that representations, precisely because they are subjective, mental phenomena, can vary within and between people (see Chap. 1, point 3).

In contrast, everything we know about metacognitive and social-cognitive development (e.g., Brown et al., 1983; Flavell, 1985; Shantz, 1983) justifies the inference that very young children understand these facts about subjectivity and mental representation less well than we do. This is to claim not that they have no awareness at all of them (see Wellman, 1985; Wellman & Estes, 1986) but only that their knowledge in this area is still quite limited. Knowing relatively little as yet about subjectivity and mental representation but having learned that things are normally either this way or that but not both at once, 3-year-olds may find such seemingly contradictory dual coding unnatural, perhaps even unthinkable. As a result, when faced with the objective need to attribute two mutually incompatible or contradictory properties or identities to the same stimulus at the very same point in time, they may only focus on and encode whichever one of the two happens to be the more cognitively salient at that moment. For them, the stimulus then "is" that one thing.

This hypothesized tendency to avoid such dual coding may also be reinforced by the child's early word-learning strategies. Markman (1984) has argued that, when first acquiring category terms, young children seem to follow a learning strategy she calls "the assumption of mutual exclusivity." That is, the child assumes that category terms are mutually exclusive and that, consequently, only one category term can be applied to any one object. This assumption would be helpful in early word learning because it would prevent the child from entertaining the hypothesis that both "dog" and "cat," say, could refer to the same animal. If the assumption were still partly active at age 3, however, it might contribute to the single-coding tendency hypothesized here. An important task for future research is to find ways to test our dual-coding hypothesis more directly.

MIDDLE CHILDHOOD

It follows from the hypothesis just proposed that, as children acquire a better understanding of subjectivity and mental representation, both simple appearance-reality problems and simple Level 2 perspective-taking problems should begin to make sense to them and become easily soluble. In the following chapter we hypothesize that their developing understanding of the pretend-real distinction may also help them understand appearance-reality and appearance-appearance (perspective-taking) distinctions. Whether or not these hypotheses are correct, there is abundant evidence from both previous and present studies that simple problems of both kinds do become increasingly easy to comprehend and solve as youngsters approach the middle childhood years. Children 4 and 5 years are considerably more competent at simple Level 2 PT tasks than are children of 3 (e.g., Flavell, Flavell, Green, & Wilcox, 1980, 1981). More generally, there is evidence that "around the ages of 4 to 6 years the ability to represent the relationship between two or more persons' epistemic states emerges and becomes firmly established" (Wimmer & Perner, 1983, p. 104). Similarly, performance on standard AR tasks improves significantly between 3 and 5 years in both American and Chinese children (Flavell, Flavell, & Green, 1983; Flavell, Zhang, Zou, Dong, & Qi, 1983). Finally, the 6–7-year-olds tested in the present Study 7 showed near ceiling performance on both kinds of problems. Study 7 clearly showed that, unlike many young early childhood subjects, young middle-childhood subjects can consistently report realities when realities are requested and appearances when appearances are requested, whether the appearances be from their own or another person's viewing position.

However, the data from Studies 5–7 also show that the development of appearance-reality-related competence is by no means completed by 6–7 years. These data indicate that the ability to identify on request stimuli exhibiting discrepancies ($A \neq R$) and equivalences ($A = R$) between appearance and reality is still fragile and task dependent at this age. On one very easy looking task calling for this ability, 6–7-year-olds performed well (Study 7). On three others, however, children of this age performed surprisingly poorly (Studies 5 and 6). They seem to find it particularly difficult to talk about appearances, realities, and appearance-reality relations ($A = R$, $A \neq R$), even briefly and minimally. They often fail to refer to appearances, realities, and appearance-reality relations when asked to explain why this chosen stimulus exhibits an appearance-reality discrepancy or that one presents an appearance-reality equivalence, even when the stimulus choices themselves have been correct. They also tend not to mention them when asked to administer the very sorts of standard AR tasks they find so easy, as subjects, to solve—even after the experimenter has explained and repeatedly demonstrated the administration procedure. As indicated at the conclusion of Study 7, we believe these difficulties in verbal labeling and nonverbal identification at least partly reflect genuine conceptual difficulties. Many subjects of this age simply seem unable to think about notions of "looks like," "really and truly," "looks different from the way it really and truly is," and so on in the abstract, metaconceptual way that older subjects can. Although they can identify concrete examples of the first and second of these notions quite easily and of the third with more difficulty, they appear to lack the knowledge and ability to reflect on and talk about— indeed, often even mention—the notions themselves.

ADOLESCENCE AND ADULTHOOD

The data from Study 5 give evidence of considerable development in this area subsequent to early middle childhood. These data suggest that 11–12-year-olds, and particularly college students, have acquired a substantial body of appearance-reality and appearance-reality-related knowledge that is both richly structured and highly accessible.

Rich structure.—Older subjects seem to possess abstract and general schemas for appearances, realities, and possible relations between the two. For example, they may make abstract, general statements such as, "This doesn't look like what it really is," when confronted with an appearance-reality discrepancy. These schemas permit them to identify as possible instances of the abstract category "A ≠ R" many different types of appearance-reality discrepancies, including unusual and marginal ones. They can similarly identify instances of the category "A = R" and can discriminate them from instances of A ≠ R. They can also recognize subtle distinctions among appearance-reality displays. In particular, they are able to identify and differentiate among realistic-looking nonfake objects (ordinary instances of A = R), realistic-looking fake objects ("good fake" instances of A ≠ R), nonrealistic-looking fakes ("poor fake" instances of A ≠ R), and even fake-looking nonfakes (unusual but also genuine instances of A ≠ R). Consistent with the data from Studies 1 and 4 suggesting that appearance-reality and perspective-taking competencies are psychologically related, older subjects often draw on their perspective-taking knowledge when thinking and talking about appearance-reality phenomena. For example, they comment spontaneously on how the appearance of a given stimulus—and therefore, perhaps, the observable appearance-reality relation—may vary with the observer's prior knowledge, previous viewing experience, or present viewing position. Finally, not only can they identify the appearances and the appearance-reality discrepancies presented to them, but they can also reproduce them, change them, or even create new ones. That is, their knowledge in this area is generative and creative as well as rich.

High accessibility.—The appearance-reality knowledge of older subjects is also more accessible, in the sense of being both (*a*) easily elicited by instructions and task materials and (*b*) readily available to conscious reflection and verbal elaboration ("metaconceptual"). As to *a*, vague instructions and a few concrete examples suffice to activate their appearance-reality knowledge; they require little help from the task materials or the experimenter. As to *b*, older subjects can describe in detail what they know and think about appearance-reality phenomena. They readily talk about their own and other people's mental events, including the expectations and inferences an object's appearance would stimulate in an observer.

X. SPECULATIONS

In this chapter we move away from the data to speculate further concerning (a) what might mediate or bring about young children's initial knowledge of the appearance-reality distinction and (b) what the subsequent development of this knowledge might mediate.

WHAT MEDIATES INITIAL KNOWLEDGE

We have already hypothesized (Chap. 9) that a developing dual-coding ability, resulting from an increasing awareness of subjectivity and mental representations, helps young children understand how something could simultaneously have two seemingly incompatible properties or identities: one apparent to the self and the other real (in appearance-reality situations) or one apparent to the self and the other apparent to another person (in Level 2 perspective-taking situations). We speculate further that such dual coding may first occur, not in these two situations, but in pretend play situations.

We believe that children cognitively work with the pretend-real distinction both earlier in life and more frequently than they work with the appearance-reality and appearance-appearance (perspectival) distinctions. There is abundant research evidence that the ability and inclination to engage in pretend play first appear around 1 year of age and increase greatly during the next several years (for reviews, see Bretherton, 1984; Fein, 1981; Rubin, Fein, & Vandenberg, 1983). Moreover, an important part of what develops in this domain is the ability to differentiate, both conceptually and verbally, between what is pretend and what is real (e.g., Bretherton, 1984; Copple, Cocking, & Matthews, 1984; DiLalla & Watson, 1985; see also Field, De-Stefano & Koewler, 1982; Fisher, 1981; Golomb & Cornelius, 1977; Howes, 1985; Nicolich, 1977; Piaget, 1962; Rubin et al., 1983; Scarlett & Wolf, 1979). For example, young children become skilled both at deliberately crossing and deliberately staying within fantasy-reality boundaries. They also become adept at verbally assigning pretend identities and properties to self, playmates, actions, and objects; for example, they often say things like, "Pretend this block is a house." As the pretend-real distinction becomes conceptually clearer and more accessible to conscious reflection and verbal expression, social as well as solitary pretend play becomes possible; in its turn, repeated practice in verbally negotiating pretend play with other children undoubtedly increases the clarity and explicitness of the distinction.

Month after month of daily practice in enacting and talking about pretend play should make it progressively easier for young children to engage in dual coding in this one domain, that is, to be able to think of something as being simultaneously pretend this but really that. Once dual coding becomes sufficiently facile in this domain of childish expertise, it may become available for transfer to the closely related but less familiar domains of apparent-real and perspectival distinctions. We also presume that the aforementioned increasing awareness of subjectivity and mental representations may help mediate pretend-real dual coding as well as the other two kinds. In sum, our conjecture is that both this increased awareness and an increased facility with pretend-real dual coding help bring about a beginning understanding of appearance-reality and perspectival distinctions.

This developmental account must predict, at minimum, that young children will perform much better on tasks that test understanding of the pretend-real distinction than on otherwise similar or identical tasks that test understanding of the apparent-real distinction. Mediators must develop earlier than the things they mediate. We have very recently obtained evidence in support of this prediction from two samples of 3-year-old children (Flavell, Flavell, & Green, 1986). To illustrate the method, in one pair of near-identical tasks an experimenter pretended to eat a realistic-looking fake apple that the child had just ascertained was really a candle. Thus the object's real identity was that of a candle, and both its apparent identity and its pretend identity were that of an apple. In one part of the testing session, the child was asked what the object presently looked like and what it really and truly was (appearance-reality task); in another part of the same session, the same child was asked what the experimenter was pretending the object was and what it really and truly was (pretend-real task). Thus the two tasks were identical in every respect save for whether the children had to answer an appearance or a pretending question. Nevertheless, the children performed significantly better on pretending questions than on appearance questions; interestingly, they also performed significantly better on reality questions asked in apposition to pretending questions than on the very same reality questions asked in apposition to appearance questions. Even though the children performed much better on the pretend-real tasks than on the appearance-reality ones, average performance on the former was only about two-thirds of the tasks fully correct; thus even these tasks proved challenging to 3-year-olds.

Our conjecture that dual coding in pretend-play situations may help mediate dual coding in appearance-reality (and appearance-appearance) situations suggests two lines of future research. One is to try to find out in much greater detail than Flavell et al. (1986) have done exactly which pretend-play skills develop earlier than or concurrently with which appearance-reality skills. The other is to find out whether it is possible to help young children understand the appearance-reality distinction by showing them how it is similar to the pretend-real distinction, that is, to try to engineer in the laboratory the transfer of learning that we believe may occur spontaneously in real life development.

WHAT INCREASED KNOWLEDGE MEDIATES

We have seen that the ability to solve simple appearance-reality problems improves markedly during the preschool years and also that a substantial body of rich, explicit, and readily accessed appearance-reality knowledge is acquired during middle childhood and adolescence. We speculate that these changes make it progressively easier for the developing individual to do two very important things: (*a*) given evidence only of how something presently appears or seems, imagine that its reality could subsequently prove to be different; and (*b*) given evidence that its reality is in fact different from its present appearance, keep that reality in mind while experiencing the appearance (dual coding).

In the case of *a*, our speculation is that these changes in appearance-reality knowledge make the growing person increasingly aware that it is always possible or conceivable for things to be different than they presently seem or appear to be. In the same vein, Piaget claimed that young children often believe "that if a situation is what it is, it is so because it cannot be otherwise" (Inhelder, 1982). The growing person comes to recognize and bear in mind that illusion and error are everpresent possibilities in life and that first impressions—even very powerful and persuasive ones—might be wrong. We believe that young children are less aware than their elders of this crucially important generalization about the world both because they have experienced fewer and less varied appearance-reality discrepancies and because they are less able and disposed to reflect on the discrepancies they have experienced. This developmental difference may explain our tendency to think of young children as innocent, trusting, credulous, and gullible and of older children and adults as more vigilant, wary, skeptical, and critical. There are age-independent individual differences as well as developmental differences on this dimension, of course, but we find the developmental ones of particular interest.

Increasing sensitivity to the ever present possibility of appearance-reality discrepancies may serve as an insufficient but necessary condition for many important cognitive and metacognitive acquisitions. These acquisitions include the understanding that quantities are really conserved under certain transformations that make them appear to have changed (e.g., Braine & Shanks, 1965a, 1965b; Murray, 1965); that the same is true of a person's self-identity and gender identity (Harter, 1983; Trautner, 1985); that people may actually be experiencing a different emotion than the one they appear to be experiencing (Harris et al., 1986); that a speaker can deliberately lie (Wimmer, Gruber, & Perner, 1984) or inadvertently fail to say what he or she means for want of sufficient communicative ability (Beal & Flavell, 1984; Bonitatibus & Flavell, 1985; Olson & Torrence, 1983; Robinson, Goelman, & Olson, 1983); that something is other than it should be on moral, conventional, practical, aesthetic, or other grounds; and that one can have the feeling that one is comprehending, communicating, learning, remembering, and so on something adequately but not really be doing so (e.g., Flavell, 1985, chaps. 4, 7). Understanding the concepts denoted by "opinion," "impression," "hypothesis," "judgment," "belief," "assumption," "guess," "inference," and of course "appearance" and "reality" should also presuppose a sensitivity to appearance-reality discrepancies. We believe with Piaget (Piaget & Inhelder, 1969) that decentration from one's present perspective plays a key role in the development of both social and nonsocial cognition and would further argue that decentration largely means going beyond initial appearances.

As to b, our dual-coding hypothesis asserts that young children have difficulty representing something as simultaneously appearing X and really being Y even when, as in our simple appearance-reality tasks, they have just been shown that it is really Y. They may be able to say that the stimulus was Y previously and will be Y again but still not be able to represent it as really Y now while it appears X. This cognitive limitation may have unsuspected but important influences on children's socioemotional lives. For example, this limitation may make it even more difficult than it otherwise would be for them to entertain the possibility that they continue to be really loved and accepted by their parents during periods when they feel unloved and rejected. Similarly, this limitation may make it harder than it otherwise would be for them not to feel frightened of currently perceived or thought of scary things that they have previously learned are not dangerous or not real (masks, monsters, shadows in the bedroom, etc.). Indeed, some of their "working through" of fears by acting out or otherwise cognitively reinstating something that frightens them may succeed because it helps them represent that thing's benign reality while experiencing its scary appearance.

It is of course true for people of any age and level of cognitive maturity that such negative feelings may override the person's knowledge that these feelings are not really justified. On the other hand, being able actively to represent and to be intellectually reassured by the known reality while experiencing the affect-laden appearance sometimes helps; it may at least permit one to act adaptively even when it does not wholly neutralize the negative feelings.

In summary, we believe that being able to represent reality and appearance simultaneously can be a useful instrument of "hot" socioemotional adaptation as well as of "cold" cognitive adaptation. We further speculate that some of young children's socioemotional behavior may be partly explained by the fact that they have not yet acquired this instrument.

REFERENCES

Austin, J. L. (1962). *Sense and sensibilia.* New York: Oxford University Press.

Beal, C. R., & Flavell, J. H. (1984). Development of the ability to distinguish communicative intention and literal message meaning. *Child Development,* **55,** 920–928.

Bonitatibus, G. J., & Flavell, J. H. (1985). The effect of presenting a message in written form on young children's ability to evaluate its communicative adequacy. *Developmental Psychology,* **21,** 455–461.

Braine, M. D. S., & Shanks, B. L. (1965a). The conservation of a shape property and a proposal about the origin of the conservations. *Canadian Journal of Psychology,* **19,** 197–207.

Braine, M. D. S., & Shanks, B. L. (1965b). The development of conservation of size. *Journal of Verbal Learning and Verbal Behavior,* **4,** 227–242.

Bretherton, I. (1984). *Symbolic play: The development of social understanding.* New York: Academic Press.

Brown, A. L., Bransford, J. D., Ferrara, R. A., & Campione, J. C. (1983). Learning, remembering, and understanding. In J. H. Flavell & E. M. Markman (Eds.), P. H. Mussen (Series Ed.), *Handbook of child psychology: Vol. 3. Cognitive development* (pp. 77–166). New York: Wiley.

Chandler, M., & Boyce M. (1982). Social-cognitive development. In B. B. Wolman (Ed.), *Handbook of developmental psychology* (pp. 387–402). Englewood Cliffs, NJ: Prentice-Hall.

Copple, C. E., Cocking, R. R., & Matthews, W. S. (1984). Objects, symbols, and substitutes: The nature of the cognitive activity during symbolic play. In T. D. Yawkey & A. D. Pellegrini (Eds.), *Child's play: Developmental and applied* (pp. 105–123). Hillsdale, NJ: Erlbaum.

Daehler, M. W. (1970). Children's manipulation of illusory and ambiguous stimuli, discriminative performance, and implications for conceptual development. *Child Development,* **41,** 225–241.

DeVries, R. (1969). Constancy of generic identity in the years three to six. *Monographs of the Society for Research in Child Development,* **34**(3, Serial No. 127).

DiLalla, L. F., & Watson, M. W. (1985, April). *Differentiation of fantasy and reality in preschoolers.* Paper presented at the meeting of the Society for Research in Child Development, Toronto.

Elkind, D. (1966). Conservation across illusory transformations in young children. *Acta Psychologica,* **25,** 389–400.

Fein, G. G. (1981). Pretend play in childhood: An integrative review. *Child Development,* **52,** 1095–1118.

Field, T., DeStefano, L., & Koewler, J. H., III. (1982). Fantasy play of toddlers and preschoolers. *Developmental Psychology,* **18,** 503–508.

Fisher, L. A. (1981). *Differentiation between fantasy and reality in preschoolers.* Unpublished senior's thesis, Brandeis University, Waltham, MA.

Flavell, J. H. (1985). *Cognitive development* (rev. ed.). Englewood Cliffs, NJ: Prentice-Hall.

Flavell, J. H., Everett, B. A., Croft, K., & Flavell, E. R. (1981). Young children's knowledge about visual perception: Further evidence for the Level 1–Level 2 distinction. *Developmental Psychology, 17*, 99–103.

Flavell, J. H., Flavell, E. R., & Green, F. L. (1983). Development of the appearance-reality distinction. *Cognitive Psychology, 15*, 95–120.

Flavell, J. H., Flavell, E. R., & Green, F. L. (1986). *Young children's knowledge about the apparent-real and the pretend-real distinction.* Manuscript submitted for publication.

Flavell, J. H., Flavell, E. R., Green, F. L., & Wilcox, S. A. (1980). Young children's knowledge about visual perception: Effect of observer's distance from target on perceptual clarity of target. *Developmental Psychology, 16*, 10–12.

Flavell, J. H., Flavell, E. R., Green, F. L., & Wilcox, S. A. (1981). The development of three spatial perspective-taking rules. *Child Development, 52*, 356–358.

Flavell, J. H., & Markman, E. M. (Eds.), Mussen, P. H. (Series Ed.). (1983). *Handbook of child psychology: Vol. 3. Cognitive development.* New York: Wiley.

Flavell, J. H., Zhang, X.-D., Zou, H., Dong, Q., & Qi, S. (1983). A comparison between the development of the appearance-reality distinction in the People's Republic of China and the United States. *Cognitive Psychology, 15*, 459–466.

Gelman, R. (1979). Preschool thought. *American Psychologist, 34*, 900–905.

Golomb, C., & Cornelius, C. B. (1977). Symbolic play and its cognitive significance. *Developmental Psychology, 13*, 246–252.

Harris, P. L., Donnelly, K., Guz, G. R., & Pitt-Watson, R. (1986). Children's understanding of the distinction between real and apparent emotion. *Child Development, 57*, 895–909.

Harter, S. (1983). Developmental perspectives on the self-system. In E. M. Hetherington (Ed.), P. H. Mussen (Series Ed.), *Handbook of child psychology: Vol. 4. Socialization, personality, and social development* (pp. 275–385). New York: Wiley.

Howes, C. (1985). Sharing fantasy: Social pretend play in toddlers. *Child Development, 56*, 1253–1258.

Inhelder, B. (1982). Outlook. In S. Modgil & C. Modgil (Eds.), *Jean Piaget: Consensus and controversy* (pp. 411–417). New York: Praeger.

King, W. L. (1971). A nonarbitrary behavioral criterion for conservation of illusion-distorted length in five-year-olds. *Journal of Experimental Child Psychology, 11*, 171–181.

Kuhn, D. (1984). Cognitive development. In M. H. Bornstein & M. E. Lamb (Eds.), *Developmental psychology: An advanced textbook* (pp. 133–180). Hillsdale, NJ: Erlbaum.

Langer, J., & Strauss, S. (1972). Appearance, reality and identity. *Cognition, 1*, 105–128.

Markman, E. M. (1984). The acquisition and hierarchical organization of categories by children. In C. Sophian (Ed.), *Origins of cognitive skills* (pp. 371–406). Hillsdale, NJ: Erlbaum.

Murray, F. B. (1965). Conservation of illusion-distorted lengths and areas by primary school children. *Journal of Educational Psychology, 56*, 62–66.

Murray, F. B. (1968). Phenomenal-real discrimination and the conservation of illusion-distorted length. *Canadian Journal of Psychology, 22*, 114–121.

Nicolich, L. (1977). Beyond sensorimotor intelligence: Assessment of symbolic maturity through analysis of pretend play. *Merrill-Palmer Quarterly, 23*, 89–101.

Olson, D. R., & Torrence, N. G. (1983). Literacy in cognitive development: A conceptual transformation in the early school years. In S. Meadows (Ed.), *Developing thinking: Approaches to children's cognitive development.* London: Methuen.

Piaget, J. (1962). *Play, dreams, and imitation.* New York: Norton.

Piaget, J., & Inhelder, B. (1969). *The psychology of the child.* New York: Basic.

Robinson, E. J., Goelman, H., & Olson, D. R. (1983). Children's understanding of the relation between expressions (what was said) and intentions (what was meant). *British Journal of Developmental Psychology*, **1**, 75–86.

Rubin, K. H., Fein, G. G., & Vandenberg, B. (1983). Play. In E. M. Hetherington (Ed.), P. H. Mussen (Series Ed.), *Handbook of child psychology: Vol. 4. Socialization, personality, and social development* (pp. 693–774). New York: Wiley.

Scarlett, W. G., & Wolf, D. (1979). When it's only make-believe: The construction of a boundary between fantasy and reality in story-telling. *New Directions for Child Development*, **6**, 29–40.

Selman, R. L. (1980). *The growth of interpersonal understanding.* New York: Academic Press.

Shantz, C. U. (1983). Social cognition. In J. H. Flavell & E. M. Markman (Eds.), P. H. Mussen (Series Ed.), *Handbook of child psychology: Vol. 3. Cognitive development* (pp. 495–555). New York: Wiley.

Taylor, M., & Flavell, J. H. (1984). Seeing and believing: Children's understanding of the distinction between appearance and reality. *Child Development*, **55**, 1710–1720.

Trautner, H. M. (1985, April). *The significance of the appearance-reality distinction for the development of gender constancy.* Paper presented at the meeting of the Society for Research in Child Development, Toronto.

Tronick, E., & Hershenson, M. (1979). Size-distance perception in preschool children. *Journal of Experimental Child Psychology*, **27**, 166–184.

Wellman, H. M. (1985). The origins of metacognition. In D. L. Forrest-Pressley, G. E. MacKinnon, & T. G. Waller (Eds.), *Metacognition, cognition, and human performance.* New York: Academic Press.

Wellman, H. M., & Estes, D. (1986). Early understanding of mental entities: A reexamination of childhood realism. *Child Development*, **57**, 910–923.

Wimmer, H., Gruber, S., & Perner, J. (1984). Young children's conception of lying: Lexical realism–moral subjectivism. *Journal of Experimental Child Psychology*, **37**, 1–30.

Wimmer, H., & Perner, J. (1983). Beliefs about beliefs: Representation and constraining function of wrong beliefs in young children's understanding of deception. *Cognition*, **13**, 103–128.

ACKNOWLEDGMENTS

This research was supported by National Institute of Child and Human Development grant HD 09814. We are very grateful to the children, teachers, and parents of Bing School of Stanford and other Bay Area schools whose cooperation made these studies possible. We are also indebted to Marjorie Taylor, Bradford Pillow, Ellen Markman, and other colleagues and students for their helpful suggestions over the course of this project.

THE BREADTH OF THE APPEARANCE-REALITY DISTINCTION

COMMENTARY BY MALCOLM W. WATSON

Investigators must go against the trend of current wisdom when they argue that preschool children have a deficiency in their understanding of reality and then claim that this deficiency is not due to hidden task demands or to a lack of training (see Gelman, 1979). Yet that is what Flavell, Green, and Flavell, the authors of this *Monograph,* have done, and they have accomplished it with refreshing elegance by testing good ideas using simple materials and straightforward procedures.

This *Monograph* is a discussion of seven studies that extend the research the authors have reported elsewhere concerning children's developing ability to distinguish appearance from reality in visual tasks and with real objects (Flavell, 1986; Flavell, Flavell, & Green, 1983; Taylor & Flavell, 1984). Three major objectives were accomplished. First, the authors attempted (and in some cases nearly bent over backward) to simplify the tasks they had used previously to assess whether 3-year-olds could distinguish the appearance of objects from their real identity and real attributes so that unnecessary demand characteristics were removed. They used two methods: (1) making tasks easier in terms of less verbal demands, lighter memory load, and increased perceptual cues available to the children and (2) giving children direct training on the tasks before presenting the tests. In general, "easier" tasks were easier for the 3-year-olds, but their performance still did not improve in any impressive way and did not reach the ceiling levels shown by older children. Likewise, the training procedures had no substantial effects in improving the performance of the children on the tests. In spite of lingering doubts in my mind regarding this counterintuitive evidence that youngsters cannot understand some of these easy distinctions, I would conclude that a genuine lack of understanding in 3-year-olds is the most parsimonious explanation.

Second, the authors assessed the further development of the ability to understand appearance-reality distinctions from late preschool years to early adulthood. These findings round out the picture of this line of development. Third, they also assessed children's concurrent perspective-taking ability and found that appearance-reality distinctions and perspective taking were related.

Their results should be important to investigators in many diverse areas in which a concern for children's perception and understanding of reality is central. The authors noted several of those areas, and, later on, I will discuss the relation of their research to some of these domains. However, the value of this research depends on the validity and generalizability of the current findings.

Validity of Findings

The most critical question that might arise is whether 3-year-olds are really incapable of the differentiations that they were asked to make. Some of the results indeed seem almost incredible. For example, children often reported that a cloth that smelled like an orange really was an orange. Were there not some other task demands that were missed by the researchers in spite of their efforts to eliminate such artifacts? One way to reduce task demands is to simplify the questioning. Children could be asked questions concerning either appearance or reality separately rather than in combination and questions concerning what the object was before a change in appearance was made and what made it change. The authors did, in fact, ask questions such as these and still obtained answers that showed evidence of a lack of understanding. As the authors note, children may expect that an object can be only one thing regardless of changing attributes and conditions, and they may concentrate on discovering what that single thing is. Thus they may think that the experimenter wants only one constant answer and, therefore, choose either the appearance answer or the real identity answer despite changing questions. One way to assess this possibility would be to ask children questions concerning their understanding of whether objects can have multiple attributes and can change conditions (e.g., How is this object both like a cloth and like an orange? Can it be both things at the same time?). When the authors did ask children what an object was or what attribute it had previously and what it would be again (e.g., What color was the object before it was covered by a colored filter? What color will it be again when the filter is removed?), children generally gave correct answers.

Although the authors provide strong evidence for a valid lack of understanding in 3-year-olds, they treat the tasks they have devised as the core tasks in an understanding of appearance and reality. Yet they have made the tasks quite narrow. These studies may indicate only one aspect of this understanding—an aspect that young preschoolers indeed are lacking. But perhaps children's correct answers on some of the related questions indicate earlier steps in their gradual understanding of the appearance-reality distinction.

An additional caveat taken from this research that applies to all attempts to reduce task demands is that by simplifying tasks, especially by eliminating apparent verbal demands, the revised tasks often bring their own new demands, which may be more difficult than those a researcher is trying to eliminate. Verbal tasks may not necessarily be the most difficult for young children.

Generalizability of the Explanation for Findings

The authors hypothesize that, in order for young children to distinguish appearance from reality in the types of tasks used, they must develop a dual coding ability. By this is meant that children can hold two seemingly incompatible properties or identities in their minds simultaneously and can apply both properties to the same object or can recognize that one property is perceived or represented by the self and another property is perceived or represented by another person. In other words, as in other examples of the ability to decentrate, children learn to focus on two or more properties of an object and coordinate these various properties.

One finding in this research provides some unexpected evidence that 3-year-olds lack this dual coding capacity. For example, when asked what a sponge looked like when in reality it looked like a rock, 3-year-olds would often answer that it looked like a sponge. They seemed to focus on what they knew it was rather than on what would be an appropriate answer to the question. Their answers contradict the common view that young children invariably will respond to the perceptual cues in their environment rather than to internal logic. In these studies, children showed a centration either on perceptual cues (phenomenism) for reality questions or on internal logic (intellectual realism) for object identity questions. They were not controlled simply by perceptual cues but could answer either way equally well; however, they acted as if they could not consider both answers simultaneously, thus implying a lack of a dual coding capacity of some sort.

An explanation involving dual coding is consistent with research in related domains in which children must make judgments about what is real and what is only an appearance. In our research on children's developing understanding of social role relations (Watson, 1984; Watson & Amgott-Kwan, 1983; Watson & Fischer, 1980), we found that 3- and 4-year-olds could not understand how two roles could be held simultaneously by the same person. For example, these children could not understand that a person could be both a doctor and a father or both a father and a grandfather. Between 4 and 6 years of age, children showed a transition step in understanding. They could discuss or act out in their role playing a person changing from a father to a doctor or a father to a grandfather, but they still could not understand that the person could be in both roles simultaneously. At about 6–7 years of age, children could fully understand this role intersection, in which one person could be in both roles simultaneously. This development in role understanding seems to parallel in both the ages and the underlying process the changing understanding of appearance and reality that this *Monograph* describes. In both domains, it seems as though children can focus on one property (of either an object or a person) at a time but cannot code both properties (appearance and identity in one case, two separate roles in another case) simultaneously until about 6 years of age.

This *Monograph* also reports that children could say what the real color of an object was before it was changed and what it would be again without the filter in place even though they could not consider the apparent color and the underlying real color of the object simultaneously. This finding sounds strikingly similar to the transition step in role understanding in which children could understand how a person's role changed from one category to another even though the person was not seen as occupying both roles simultaneously.

In another related domain, children have been found to develop gradually over the preschool years the ability to differentiate fantasy from reality in their pretense (DiLalla & Watson, 1985; Morison & Gardner, 1978; Scarlett & Wolf, 1979). The evidence suggests that children first learn to differentiate the two realms of fantasy and reality and then later are able to integrate the two so that both can be considered nearly simultaneously. In our research (DiLalla & Watson, 1985), we speculated that children first view all events as occurring in one temporal sequence. Only one event occurs at a time. Gradually the child comes to change this view to one in which fantasy and reality events occur in parallel temporal sequences, such that both fantasy and reality events can occur simultaneously. The child need not lose touch with the world of reality while engaging in the parallel world of fantasy. For example, while playing house, the child can step out of the fantasy to handle an interruption or to narrate the story and then step back in again. Again, similar to the findings in this *Monograph*, children show evidence for this ability to integrate both realms (or dual coding capability, if you will) at about 6 years of age.

Another example of a related domain of development comes from recent research on how children interpret television programs. For example, Leary (1985) assessed preschoolers' difficulty differentiating fantasy and reality in television characters, and Paget, Kritt, and Bergemann (1984) assessed children's reaction to television commercials in terms of the acting involved and the thoughts and intent of the characters and producers. By using the results and the dual coding explanation from this *Monograph* as a guide, investigators might be able to expand and more fully explain our understanding of children's reactions to television.

These examples are given as suggestions of how the authors' hypothesized explanation of a dual coding capability developing sometime between 3 and 6 years of age is an explanation that is generalizable to several related areas of development, which also include a regard for the child's understanding of appearances and reality.

Relation of Appearance-Reality Distinction to Pretense

The authors discussed the likely relation between children's developing ability at making appearance-reality distinctions and their ability at making fantasy-reality distinctions in pretend play. Based on questions they asked concerning children's understanding of pretense, they concluded that children are able to engage in dual coding in this domain first, owing to extensive practice and exposure, before engaging in dual coding when dealing with visual perspective tasks. I agree that there is likely a strong relation between these two domains; however, it is more likely that there is a parallel development between the two domains than that one is a simple precursor to the other.

It is true that pretend play normally begins early in the second year of a child's life at a time when there is little evidence for their ability to make appearance-reality distinctions. Nevertheless, pretending also develops gradually throughout the preschool years by way of a sequence of steps or abilities (Rubin, Fein, & Vandenberg, 1983; Scarlett & Wolf, 1979; Watson & Jackowitz, 1984). The ability of children to control the distinctions between fantasy and reality are also gradual in developing, as was discussed above. For example, even though young children will pretend that rocks are food without trying to eat them, when they have created a complex or frightening pretense situation, they often get confused about the boundaries of fantasy (DiLalla & Watson, 1985; Scarlett & Wolf, 1979). I am certain the authors do not believe that development in either domain is an all-or-nothing affair, but, by focusing on some of the earliest incidences of children using pretense and differentiating fantasy from reality, they have given the impression that they believe that skill in this one domain develops fully, followed by development in the other domain. A better view might be that in each domain children are gradually and in parallel fashion developing the ability to differentiate appearance from reality.

Another aspect of the relation between the pretense realm and the visual perspective realm is worthy of further study. Some research has indicated that children in different cultures vary widely in the amount and quality of pretend play that they show at different ages (Feitelson, 1977). In cultures in which pretense is not as prevalent, will children show a differentiation of appearance and reality as early as the authors have found in their research? Cross-cultural comparisons of the relations between pretense skills and ability to distinguish appearance and reality could help determine whether pretense is a precursor to later appearance-reality distinctions.

Sequence of Development and an Integration of Domains

The results of both the research presented in this *Monograph* and related research from other domains point to a general sequence of development that seems to apply to many related areas of development (e.g., appearance-reality distinctions, pretend play, fantasy-reality differentiation, perspective taking, and children's reactions to television). First, young preschoolers seem to develop a beginning knowledge regarding what is real and what is only apparent or pretense, and they use this ability in practical situations. However, they have a difficult time coordinating the two seemingly conflicting sides. Second, older preschoolers and younger school-aged children develop the ability to coordinate the two sides (i.e., dual encoding capability) and can handle challenges that experimenters throw at them. The ability to handle challenges to one's understanding may indeed be strong evidence for a newly developed level of understanding. Third, school-aged children and adolescents develop the additional ability to explain and demonstrate their knowledge to someone else. They show that they can monitor what they know and consciously find relations between specific incidences.

In an impressive way, the authors have also demonstrated their own integration of domains by providing evidence for the connections between their work on appearance-reality distinctions and their earlier work on perspective-taking abilities and the development of metacognition (Flavell, 1979; Flavell, Flavell, Green, & Wilcox, 1981). In the *Monograph*, they discuss the relations between the appearance-reality distinctions and perspective taking. Also, it should be clear that the last step of development, as reviewed above, is in fact a description of a metacognitive knowledge that emerges after children have developed a practical skill and dual coding capability in handling the appearance-reality distinctions.

In conclusion, the sequence of development and the ties between areas elucidated in this *Monograph* make a most valuable contribution by showing us in what direction to go if we want to gain a complete picture of how children develop knowledge of fantasy and reality and of other important related domains.

References

DiLalla, L. F., & Watson, M. W. (1985, April). *Differentiation of fantasy and reality in preschoolers.* Paper presented at the meeting of the Society for Research in Child Development, Toronto.

Feitelson, D. (1977). Cross-cultural studies of representational play. In B. Tizard & D. Harvey (Eds.), *Biology of play* (pp. 6–14). Philadelphia: Lippincott.

Flavell, J. H. (1979). Metacognition and cognitive monitoring: A new area of cognitive-developmental inquiry. *American Psychologist, 34,* 906–911.

Flavell, J. H. (1986). The development of children's knowledge about the appearance-reality distinction. *American Psychologist, 41,* 418–425.

Flavell, J. H., Flavell, E. R., & Green, F. L. (1983). Development of the appearance-reality distinction. *Cognitive Psychology, 15,* 95–120.

Flavell, J. H., Flavell, E. R., Green, F. L., & Wilcox, S. A. (1981). The development of three spatial perspective-taking rules. *Child Development, 52,* 356–358.

Gelman, R. (1979). Preschool thought. *American Psychologist, 34,* 900–905.

Leary, A. (1985, April). *Young children's judgments of the fictional/nonfictional status of television programming.* Paper presented at the meeting of the Society for Research in Child Development, Toronto.

Morison, P., & Gardner, H. (1978). Dragons and dinosaurs: On distinguishing the realms of reality and fantasy. *Child Development, 49,* 642–648.

Paget, K. F., Kritt, D., & Bergemann, L. (1984). Understanding strategic interactions in television commercials: A developmental study. *Journal of Applied Developmental Psychology, 5,* 145–161.

Rubin, K. H., Fein, G. G., & Vandenberg, B. (1983). Play. In E. M. Hetherington (Ed.), P. H. Mussen (Series Ed.), *Handbook of child psychology: Vol 4. Socialization, personality, and social development* (pp. 693–774). New York: Wiley.

Scarlett, W. G., & Wolf, D. (1979). When it's only make-believe: The construction of a boundary between fantasy and reality storytelling. *New Directions for Child Development,* No. **6,** 29–40.

Taylor, M., & Flavell, J. H. (1984). Seeing and believing: Children's understanding of the distinction between appearance and reality. *Child Development, 55,* 1710–1720.

Watson, M. W. (1984). Development of social role understanding. *Developmental Review, 4,* 192–213.

Watson, M. W., & Amgott-Kwan, T. (1983). Transitions in children's understanding of parental roles. *Developmental Psychology, 19,* 659–666.

Watson, M. W., & Fischer, K. W. (1980). Development of social roles in elicited and spontaneous behavior during the preschool years. *Developmental Psychology, 16,* 483–494.

Watson, M. W., & Jackowitz, E. R. (1984). Agents and recipient objects in the development of early symbolic play. *Child Development, 55,* 1091–1097.

[**Malcolm W. Watson** (Ph.D. 1977, University of Denver) is associate professor of psychology at Brandeis University. His published research is primarily in the areas of children's play and symbol use and in children's developing concepts of social and family role relations and includes the review Development of social role understanding, *Developmental Review*, 1984, **4,** 192–213.]

THE APPEARANCE-REALITY DISTINCTION—MORE THAN MEETS THE EYE

COMMENTARY BY JOSEPH C. CAMPIONE

This *Monograph,* by Flavell, Green, and Flavell, touches on a number of subthemes that can be read and appreciated at a variety of levels. At a basic level, the programmatic series of studies provides a thoughtful extension of prior work by Flavell and his colleagues on the development of the appearance-reality distinction and perspective-taking skills. The empirical results give us a rich description of the course of development. Seen in this light, the overall program of research can be regarded as a paradigmatic case of a group of researchers employing a variety of experimental approaches to paint a detailed picture of developmental change over a wide age range. That contribution is interesting and important in its own right, but there is more than that to be gleaned from the report, which can also be read at a more general level as providing a window on cognitive development in a wider sense. Not only do the authors produce a description of development, but they also point to some of the factors that go along with and produce that development. Going beyond this, they also argue persuasively for the importance of appearance-reality and perspective-taking skills as fundamental building blocks, or conceptual foundations, of cognitive development.

The starting point of this research is the well-documented finding that preschool children have considerable difficulty dealing with the fact that objects can lend themselves to multiple representations, for example, that they may not be what they appear to be (appearance-reality; see, e.g., Braine & Shanks, 1965a, 1965b; Flavell, Flavell, & Green, 1983) or that they may be seen differently by different observers (perspective-taking; e.g., Flavell, Everett, Croft, & Flavell, 1981). An object's appearance varies across observers; and an object's appearance can be downright misleading. While these results are classic ones that precede the immediate research program, Flavell and his collaborators have greatly extended the empirical foundations and have made significant strides toward integrating the findings into an overall theoretical framework.

For example, Flavell et al. (1983) have pointed out that 3-year-olds evidence their difficulties with the appearance-reality distinction in two distinct ways. When confronted with objects whose appearance and reality differ, they sometimes show *phenomenism* error patterns. As a prototypical example, when viewing a white object through a green filter, they fail to distinguish the object's apparent color from its true color by reporting that it is truly green. Alternatively, there are occasions on which they show *intellectual realism* error patterns. In another standard example, they might assert that a candle that looks like an apple both appears to be and truly is a candle. In the tasks that Flavell, Green, and Flavell term "standard Appearance-Reality (AR) tasks," these errors are greatly reduced by age 5 and virtually eliminated by age 7. Three-year-olds appear to know something about the appearance-reality distinction but much less than their slightly older counterparts. In addition, in the work reported in the *Monograph,* Flavell, Green, and Flavell provide evidence that appearance-reality and perspective-taking skills themselves have important overlaps, a finding that advances our understanding of both areas and allows the development of more general theory.

The Course of Development

These facts are clear, but what of the interpretation of this developmental trend? Is there some fairly dramatic growth taking place during the preschool years, or is it the case that the experimental procedures used in the standard tasks mask the competence of the younger samples? One way of addressing this issue is to supplement the data obtained in the standard tasks by asking how difficult it is to reduce the performance differences through manipulations designed to induce better performance from the young. The notion here is the traditional one of readiness—even if young children cannot solve a task readily on their own, how close are they to being able to do so? As one example, in some of our own work (Brown & Campione, 1984; Campione & Brown, in press), we have supplemented information on individual's entering performance within a number of domains with estimates of how much help they need before they can deal with previously insoluble problems. The amount-of-help metric provides more predictive information about individuals' later performance than does the initial performance level. The conclusion is that individuals' responsiveness to input is an indication of readiness, which is a better measure of relative status than the original performance estimate.

Ease of bringing about change indicates that the necessary competencies are close to the surface rather than being deeply buried or nonexistent. There are by now many examples of cases in which somewhat simple manipulations have resulted in young children's being able to demonstrate the possession of considerably more competence than they had originally been thought to have. The major techniques that have been used are to strip away all nonessential task requirements in order to reveal the task's cognitive demands in the simplest possible form and to situate the experiment in familiar settings (Brown, Bransford, Ferrara, & Campione, 1983; Flavell & Wohlwill, 1969; Gelman, 1978). This approach has demonstrated early precosity in many important areas, including number skills (Gelman & Gallistel, 1978), communicative competence (Shatz, 1978), understanding of causality (Bullock, Gelman, & Baillargeon, 1982; Shultz, 1982), deployment of memory strategies (Brown & DeLoache, 1978; DeLoache, Cassidy, & Brown, 1985), and so on. Indeed, as Flavell (1982) and Gelman (1983) have noted, we have for a while been inundated with glowing descriptions of the competence of the very young.

In this vein, the first four experiments in the *Monograph* include a set of extremely clever manipulations designed to induce young children to demonstrate whatever appearance-reality or perspective-taking competence they may have. The methods used to uncover this competence are based on rational analyses of the factors that might occlude its appearance in standard experimental designs. Thus, in Study 1, the authors make sure that poor performance is not an artifact of memory problems that the 3-year-olds may experience. They also make use of standard ploys by choosing objects more familiar to their subjects than those used in the standard tasks and by embedding the task in more familiar contexts. They further attempt to make the task easier for their preschoolers by reducing the information-processing requirements of the task, for example, by requiring them to answer only one question per object rather than two questions that require opposing answers. These attempts are continued in Studies 2 and 4, in which the children are given more extensive pretraining on the appearance-reality distinction, and the tasks are further designed to be more child friendly. Finally, in Study 3, the effects of detailed and explicit training on the appearance-reality distinction are investigated.

The sum, this portion of the research amounts to a set of battles between an ingenious cadre of experimenters and a set of 3-year-olds determined to communicate their deep confusion about the appearance-reality distinction. The preschoolers come away handy winners, as none of the manipulations has a significant effect. These results stand in stark contrast to those alluded to earlier. While it has become commonplace for us to discover that young children know much more than meets the eye, in the case of the appearance-reality distinction that simply does not seem to be the case.

There are, of course, problems associated with these null results. In any studies designed to enhance the performance of a group of learners, failures to effect change are difficult to interpret. Detailed, theoretically based analyses of both the experimental task requirements and the cognitive competency being assessed are necessary before we can be confident that the chosen modifications do indeed eliminate the role of extraneous factors while highlighting those targeted for study. The changes introduced by Flavell, Green, and Flavell, while reasonable, are not strongly justified in this sense. Similarly, attempts to reveal competence by reducing the information-processing demands may or may not accomplish that task. Again, what is needed is a theoretical framework within which we can evaluate the information-processing requirements of various tasks, a computation that Flavell (1978) has pointed out leaves something to be desired in terms of "inter-psychologist reliability." Which aspects of a particular experimental task do make particular demands on information-processing resources, and how can they be reduced? For example, does requiring children to answer one question rather than two really affect the information-processing requirements in an important way? Finally, the quality or power of a training program can be evaluated along many dimensions. Is the instruction aimed at the appropriate level for the learner? For example, are there additional task-related competencies that need to be considered (and possibly instilled) before the instruction can be effective (Campione & Armbruster, 1984; Campione & Brown, 1974)? Are the pedagogical principles underlying the training defensible? Obviously, unless the answers here are positive, the possibility exists that other training programs would be more effective.

These are not issues unique to this research. Essentially, attempts to improve performance can be regarded as attempts to provide supportive contexts (Brown & Reeve, in press) for learners in the form of task clarifications or modifications, provision of social or contextual support, and so on. In the field in general, the notion of supportive contexts has been used as an explanatory concept without itself being adequately explained. Much progress in our understanding of developmental issues will result when a strong theory of supportive contexts is provided. Until all this work has been done, one way around the interpretive problems is to resort to converging operations, that is, making a multifaceted series of attempts at inducing change rather than basing conclusions on only one approach. While individual studies can be faulted, it is more difficult to argue against a set of studies that converge on some conclusion. In this context, the authors are to be commended on their many and dramatic failures. One comes away convinced that their youngest subjects are truly in trouble.

Given the recalcitrance of the 3-year-olds, the next issue concerns the pattern of subsequent development. Is it fairly rapid or gradual and extended? What mediates that development, and are there any important implications of this particular developmental acquisition? What does one make of the near-ceiling performance of 6–7-year-olds on these AR and Perspective-Taking (PT) tasks? First graders report both the appearance and the reality of object properties and identities and distinguish what they see from what others see. Does this mean they command the relevant distinctions in the same way as do older children or adults? Clearly not, as the authors show in another set of comparisons.

The experimental approach taken with the first graders is the opposite of that used to tackle the 3-year-olds. Given the poor performance of the youngest samples, the question was, How difficult is it to improve on that level? In contrast, given the ceiling performance of the 7-year-olds, the issue is, How easy or difficult is it to disrupt that performance, or how much additional skill can be uncovered? Thus the "standard" tasks are used to provide only a very rough estimate of the current status of conceptual development. If children perform poorly, attempts are made to simplify the task requirements to uncover nascent abilities, or degrees of readiness, not discernible originally. Conversely, if children experience little or no difficulty with the standard tasks, the complexity of these tasks is increased, with the goal of inducing children to "stretch" their abilities and allowing us to achieve better estimates of the upper limits of current competence. In either case, the idea is not only to assess a task-specific competence level but in addition to estimate the child's current zone of proximal development (Vygotsky, 1978) or the bandwidth of the competence in question (Brown & Campione, 1978; Brown & Reeve, in press), that is, its fragility or stability across task settings.

In Studies 5 and 7, the task demands are stepped up considerably to evaluate the limits of their understanding of the relevant distinctions. First graders are asked either to administer the AR tasks they can solve (Study 7) or to make a number of fine distinctions among items designed to exhibit a number of appearance-reality relations (Study 5): true appearance equals reality items (which are what they appear to be) and three variants of appearance does not equal reality items (realistic-looking fakes; nonrealistic-looking fakes; and fake-looking nonfakes, e.g., an artificial looking real flower). Suddenly, the former experts, the first graders, become the incompetent group. While they can solve many of the appearance-reality problems, they are quite unable to administer to others the very ones they have solved. In addition, they appear quite unable to distinguish the differing appearance-reality relations. When asked to pick which of a pair of items shows the greater appearance-reality discrepancy, their choices are essentially random. Finally, when they make reasonable distinctions, they are unable to justify them adequately. Sixth graders are better able to make and defend these distinctions than are first graders, but their performance is still notably below that of college students. Investigating the performance of subjects of widely varying ages in a diverse array of task contexts makes it clear that the emergence of a rich understanding of the appearance-reality distinction is a lengthy and gradual one. It is this probing for competence across a wide age range *and* investigating that emerging competence in a variety of task settings that is surprisingly rare in the developmental literature and sets this work apart from most analyses of developmental change.

Perhaps the clearest contribution of the *Monograph* is to remind us that the fact that we can detect signs of early competence within some arena is a small part of the overall endeavor. This case history shows that the steps from early indications of understanding to a fully developed one are many, and we can come to appreciate development within a domain only when the limits of understanding are probed thoroughly throughout the course of that growth; that is, we trace not only the development of the "basic capacity" but also the bandwidths of that capacity at successive points in development. With this information in hand, we can proceed to build and evaluate theories of the developmental changes involved. Rich descriptions of development of the kind provided here are necessary precursors to theory development. Further, it is only when we have clear and detailed pictures of the development of a number of core accomplishments that we will be able to discern the more general mechanisms of growth that form the base questions of developmental psychology.

The What of Development

What is happening as children progress from 3-year-olds with at best a fragile and limited understanding of the appearance-reality distinction to college students in clear command of that distinction? What might this tell us about cognitive development more broadly? In their treatment, the authors emphasize two factors, the acquisition of relevant knowledge and the awareness of, and access to, that knowledge. It is important to emphasize, however, that the knowledge they refer to is both quite specific (they are very clear in specifying that knowledge) and at the same time of very general importance (its effects are extremely broad). In contrast to the knowledge stressed in other developmental treatments (e.g., Carey, 1985), it is relatively content free. Flavell, Green, and Flavell center on the role of metaconceptual knowledge regarding subjectivity and multiple representations. The pointer to that knowledge is based on the correlation between performance on the AR and the PT tasks. Children who correctly note that an object's reality can be different from what its appearance suggests are also likely to acknowledge the fact that an item may appear different to different observers. This suggests to the authors that a more general phenomenon is involved, namely, that both sets of judgments require that subjects appreciate the subjectivity of mental representations, with the associated possibility of multiple representations of an object or event that can vary both within and between individuals. In this view, their youngest children, forming and acting on only one encoding of the event, cannot deal with the competing, and simultaneous, experiences. Thus they are restricted to reporting only the immediate appearance of the object *or* its reality. What they see is what it is, or what it is is what they see, and never the twain shall meet.

An appreciation of this subjectivity of mental representations, moreover, can exist at many levels; it can become richer or more accessible. Flavell, Green, and Flavell are impressed with the importance of both multiple and reflective access (Pylyshyn, 1978) in mediating development, that is, the ease of retrieving relevant knowledge across tasks and the ability to step back on that knowledge and treat it as itself an object of thought. Regarding reflection, the major differences between younger and older subjects lie not only in their ability to make increasingly subtle distinctions among types of appearance-reality discrepancies but also in their ability to explicate them, to describe them abstractly, to create and explain additional ones, to use their knowledge of perspective-taking phenomena to elaborate appearance-reality experiences, and so on. These abilities are particularly clear in the case of the college student. This stress on the role of reflective access is consistent with research in the area of metacognition (Brown et al., 1983; Flavell, 1985), where heavy emphasis has been placed on the importance of children's growing awareness and conscious control of their expanding cognitive repertoires.

Interestingly, given that Flavell was primarily responsible for the introduction of Piaget's early writings to American psychology, the emphasis on reflection is also consistent with Piaget's (1976) later writings, specifically his distinction between autonomous, active, and conscious regulation. In Piaget's view, development consists of a progression from unconscious autonomous regulation, an integral part of any knowing act, to active regulation, in which the learner begins to take some, albeit limited, direct control over events through conscious regulation, in which case the learner is capable of describing his thoughts and activities to others and carrying them out exclusively on the mental plane. Conscious regulation allows the use of the skills and knowledge in the service of testing other theories and constructing other knowledge. It is, for Piaget, the basis of formal scientific reasoning.

In sum, the authors' developmental account rests on the assumed importance to both the AR and the PT tasks of the acquisition of metaconceptual knowledge regarding mental representations, along with an increasing ability to reflect on and manipulate that knowledge. As children mature, they acquire more detailed and richer knowledge about mental representations. They also become more capable of talking about and evaluating that knowledge, which in turn makes it more available for use in a wider range of situations. This then translates into the acquisition of a tool that can itself facilitate new developmental acquisitions.

Pushing this account further, the authors are able to generate several hypotheses that can help flesh out the developmental picture they are trying to paint. These have to do with the precursors to the competency that preschoolers do bring to these experiments and with mechanisms for refining their nascent understandings. First, what might be the source of the fragile knowledge that preschoolers have concerning appearance-reality phenomena? What are the precursors to even that fleeting capability? Flavell, Green, and Flavell suggest that a particularly likely candidate is pretend play, which occurs in naturalistic settings placing minimal restrictions on children and which shares with the AR and PT tasks the need to represent objects in alternative ways. According to Flavell, Green, and Flavell, children's increasing involvement in such play situations, and their need to "negotiate" them, results in their becoming increasingly aware of the possibility of dual encoding, and this increased ability to engage in active regulation forms the basis for transfer to the more complex appearance-reality and perspective-taking cases (again, it would be nice to have a clear description of the determinants of the sources of such complexity). As the multiple representation notion becomes practiced in more settings, and as individuals acquire increasing reflective access to this notion, they can call on it as a tool in many other learning situations. Again, it is interesting that Piaget regarded the ability to engage in pretend play as marking the transition from sensory-motor to symbolic thinking.

Although these claims are reasonable and elegant, the authors are aware that the argument remains quite speculative; however, the claims are testable. Much of the argument rests on the assumed overlap between the demands of the pretend play, AR, and PT tasks, and the correlational data regarding the AR and PT tasks, while supportive, are hardly sufficient. If common components do underlie performance in the various tasks, it should be possible to show that through detailed microgenetic analysis. The studies Flavell and his colleagues have done thus far indicate, for example, that considerable change takes place across fairly narrow age ranges. It seems that the next step is to sharpen that picture by investigating directly the codevelopment of the theoretically related skills through more intensive microgenetic analyses.

Also, the assumption of shared components suggests it should be possible to engineer transfer from, for example, pretend play situations to AR tasks, as the authors in fact indicate. Attempts to design training studies can be interesting theoretical exercises in their own right. They require a detailed analysis of the components of the skills under consideration, to make clear what the targets of instruction should be, and also depend on some assumptions about what the underlying learning/transfer mechanisms are so that the form of instruction can be dictated. In this regard, it is interesting to note that the suggested attempt to facilitate appearance-reality performance by capitalizing on developmentally prior pretend-play skills would not have been possible without the view that attention to dual encodings is an important component of the AR task and shared with the pretend-play task. The training manipulation that results is dictated by this theoretical position and considerably more focused than the one reported in Study 3.

Why Study Appearance-Reality?

Is there a reason developmental psychologists should be particularly interested in appearance-reality and related phenomena? Flavell, Green, and Flavell (and many others) believe that there is, and it is difficult not to agree. As discussed in the previous section, research on the appearance-reality distinction has illuminated our understanding of cognitive development in general—the account of developmental change and its mediators in this area mesh nicely with, and reinforce, similar accounts in other areas. Also, there have been many authors who have argued that an appreciation of the appearance-reality distinction does underlie other important performances; that is, it can be regarded as a conceptual foundation or motivator for other important, even stagelike, advances in thinking. The ability to note that objects' appearances and their realities may differ has been assumed by various authors to be centrally involved in the ability to conserve, where changes in the appearance of some substance are irrelevant to quantitative properties of that substance; in the ability to communicate effectively, where it is necessary to realize that messages can be perceived differently by different individuals or by a given individual in different states; in the ability to reason scientifically, where the goal is to go beyond surface appearances and uncover reality; and so on. While these are again claims in need of additional verification, there is good reason to believe that an understanding of the appearance-reality distinction will contribute significantly to our understanding of many central developmental issues. Again, it appears that the way to extend, evaluate, or attack the theory being built is through detailed microgenetic analyses of individual learners. If the theory is correct, it should be possible to make predictions about some of the changes in related cognitive performances that should result from increments in children's ability to solve and discuss appearance-reality problems. Advances in appearance-reality expertise should result in increased readiness to deal with other, theoretically specifiable, tasks.

In summary, this *Monograph* is important for both its methodological and its theoretical messages. Flavell, Green, and Flavell provide us with an extremely rich picture of the development of the appearance-reality distinction. In this, they make use of a variety of experimental approaches and tasks and provide a paradigmatic case study of how one might proceed to generate a detailed picture of development. They also go beyond their immediate data and outline a theoretical account of the basis and emergence of appearance-reality and related phenomena. This account provides important information about cognitive development in general, allows the integration of a number of different literatures and phenomena, and leads to a set of testable hypotheses that can usefully guide further research.

References

Braine, M. D. S., & Shanks, B. L. (1965a). The conservation of a shape property and a proposal about the origin of the conservations. *Canadian Journal of Psychology, 19,* 197–207.

Braine, M. D. S., & Shanks, B. L. (1965b). The development of conservation of size. *Journal of Verbal Learning and Verbal Behavior, 4,* 227–242.

Brown, A. L., Bransford, J. D., Ferrara, R. A., & Campione, J. C. (1983). Learning, remembering, and understanding. In J. H. Flavell & E. M. Markman (Eds.), P. H. Mussen (Series Ed.), *Handbook of child psychology: Vol. 3. Cognitive development* (pp. 77–166). New York: Wiley.

Brown, A. L., & Campione, J. C. (1978). Permissible inferences from cognitive training studies in developmental research. *Quarterly Newsletter of the Institute for Comparative Human Behavior, 2,* 46–53.

Brown, A. L., & Campione, J. C. (1984). Three faces of transfer: Implications for early competence, individual differences, and instruction. In M. Lamb, A. Brown, & B. Rogoff (Eds.), *Advances in developmental psychology* (Vol. 3). Hillsdale, NJ: Erlbaum.

Brown, A. L., & DeLoache, J. S. (1978). Skills, plans, and self-regulation. In R. S. Siegler (Ed.), *Children's thinking: What develops?* Hillsdale, NJ: Erlbaum.

Brown, A. L., & Reeve, R. A. (in press). Bandwidths of competence: The role of supportive contexts in learning and development. In L. S. Liben & D. H. Feldman (Eds.), *Development and learning: Conflict or congruence?* Hillsdale, NJ: Erlbaum.

Bullock, M., Gelman, R., & Baillargeon, R. (1982). The development of causal reasoning. In J. Friedman (Ed.), *The developmental psychology of time.* New York: Academic Press.

Campione, J. C., & Armbruster, B. B. (1984). An analysis of the outcomes and interventions of intervention research. In H. Mandl, N. Stein, & T. Trabasso (Eds.), *Learning and comprehension of texts.* Hillsdale, NJ: Erlbaum.

Campione, J. C., & Brown, A. L. (1974). The effects of contextual changes and degree of component mastery in transfer of training. In H. W. Reese (Ed.), *Advances in child development and behavior* (Vol. 9). New York: Academic Press.

Campione, J. C., & Brown, A. L. (in press). Dynamic assessment: One approach and some initial data. In C. S. Lidz (Ed.), *Dynamic assessment.* New York: Guilford.

Carey, S. (1985). *Conceptual change in childhood.* Cambridge, MA: MIT Press.

DeLoache, J. S., Cassidy, L., & Brown, A. L. (1985). Precursors of mnemonic strategies in very young children's memory. *Child Development,* **56,** 125–137.

Flavell, J. H. (1978). Comments. In R. S. Siegler (Ed.), *Children's thinking: What develops?* Hillsdale, NJ: Erlbaum.

Flavell, J. H. (1982). On cognitive development. *Child Development,* **53,** 1–10.

Flavell, J. H. (1985). *Cognitive development* (2d ed.). Englewood Cliffs, NJ: Prentice-Hall.

Flavell, J. H., Everett, B. A., Croft, K., & Flavell, E. R. (1981). Young children's knowledge about visual perception: Further evidence for the Level 1–Level 2 distinction. *Developmental Psychology,* **17,** 99–103.

Flavell, J. H., Flavell, E. R., & Green, F. L. (1983). Development of the appearance-reality distinction. *Cognitive Psychology,* **15,** 95–120.

Flavell, J. H., & Wohlwill, J. F. (1969). Formal and functional aspects of cognitive development. In D. Elkind & J. H. Flavell (Eds.), *Studies in cognitive development: Essays in honor of Jean Piaget.* New York: Oxford University Press.

Gelman, R. (1978). Cognitive development. *Annual Review of Psychology,* **29,** 297–332.

Gelman, R. (1983). Recent trends in cognitive development. In J. Schierer & A. Rogers (Eds.), *The G. Stanley Hall Lecture Series* (Vol. **3**). Washington, DC: American Psychological Association.

Gelman, R., & Gallistel, C. R. (1978). *The child's understanding of number.* Cambridge, MA: Harvard University Press.

Piaget, J. (1976). *The grasp of consciousness: Action and concept in the young child.* Cambridge, MA: Harvard University Press.

Pylyshyn, Z. W. (1978). When is attribution of beliefs justified? *Behavioral and Brain Sciences,* **1,** 592–593.

Shatz, M. (1978). The relationships between cognitive processes and the development of communication skills. In B. Keasey (Ed.), *Nebraska symposium on motivation.* Lincoln: University of Nebraska Press.

Shultz, T. R. (1982). Rules of causal attribution. *Monographs of the Society for Research in Child Development,* **47**(1, Serial No. 194).

Vygotsky, L. S. (1978). *Mind in society: The development of higher psychological processes* (M. Cole, V. John-Steiner, S. Scribner, & E. Souberman, Eds.). Cambridge, MA: Harvard University Press.

[**Joseph C. Campione** (Ph.D. 1965, University of Connecticut) is professor of psychology at the University of Illinois at Urbana-Champaign. His research interests are focused on theories of learning and transfer and on the development of alternative methods of assessing individual and developmental differences.]

STATEMENT OF EDITORIAL POLICY

At the beginning of each year, we plan to provide a Statement of Editorial Policy to inform authors who may be considering a submission to *Monographs.*

The *Monographs* series is one of the longest continuing publications in the field of child development. It is intended to provide for publication of significant research reports that require longer presentations than that permitted in journal-length articles. Because of its circulation (over 5,000 copies are automatically distributed) and because single copies are available through the University of Chicago Press, this archival series may offer unique publication opportunities for investigators who are completing major programmatic projects.

Longitudinal studies are a special priority for the *Monographs.* Studies that utilize successive measurements on the same subjects are of particular importance to the field of child development and for understanding developmental processes. Longitudinal studies are apt to require considerable space, not only to describe the context of the study, but also to discuss methods, data, and theoretical implications. Special consideration is also given to studies of relevance to more than one discipline. Interdisciplinary collaborative research is often particularly enlightening for understanding developmental processes. Reports of multiple experiments on a single problem are also a priority for *Monographs,* when a unified report is more suitable than a series of articles. This category of priority may involve a diversity of methods focused around a central theme or a single method for studying several variables. Still, a series of experiments that does not have a necessary unity, even though it has a programmatic thrust, would be more appropriately published as a series of articles.

Among the important priorities for *Monographs* are reports of new directions in developmental research. We hope that *Monographs* can help catalyze the initiation and development of new research areas. Several formats may be suitable, and innovation is encouraged. *Monographs* can publish the proceedings of a particularly exciting and generative conference or symposium. It is anticipated that such a collection would involve a group of scientists who link more than one discipline with one or more problem areas and a symposium discussant who would provide introductory and concluding sections. The subject matter should be of interest to a substantial number of people, and the problems discussed should be developmental and remarkably innovative for submission in this category.

Other traditional categories for publication in *Monographs* include studies of physical growth and cross-cultural studies, and this practice will continue.

A few caveats. Perhaps the most important is that Ph.D. dissertations are rarely considered appropriate submissions for *Monographs;* usually the editor returns such submission without review. There are many reasons for this policy. Most dissertations are written to demonstrate to a faculty that a student is competent. For this purpose, dissertations contain extensive reviews of the literature, tabular material, rationales for planning and execution, and lengthy discussions concerning errors, unanticipated results, and speculative applications. Most dissertations should be reduced and published as single articles.

Another caveat concerns the substantive nature of the work. Authors should ask themselves the following questions. Is the work truly developmental? Does it clearly represent the state of the art and science for reliable and valid observations, relevant controls, and data analytic procedures? Finally, as Robert Sears said of a prospective submission to *Monographs* in an editorial policy statement written in 1971, "It should be meat for a full section of a textbook chapter, not for a footnote. It should start a new field or put an end to an old one. It should be one that a *lot* of developmentalists care about and want to see some data on. A monograph should add a building block on which other researchers can step, not just an *i*-dotting or *t*-crossing of the latest fad" (Robert R. Sears, *Child Development*, 1971, **42**, 341).

Every attempt will be made to obtain at least two expert reviewers who are experienced and competent in the areas of submitted manuscripts accepted for review. Reviewers will be asked to bear the above priorities in mind as they look at a manuscript for scientific excellence and for results that will provide archival data to which other investigators will repeatedly return.

Monographs, like *Child Development*, accepts manuscripts from nonmembers of the Society for Research in Child Development as well as from members. A manuscript should be no briefer than 70 pages, including references, tables, and figures; the upper limit of 150–175 pages is somewhat more flexible because of the possibility of publishing a "double issue" *Monographs*. The style and format required by *Monographs* adheres to that of the current publication manual of the American Psychological Association (3d Ed.). *All* material should be typed double-spaced.

Potential authors may wish to consult the editor directly about matters of appropriate length, topic, and style. A more detailed "Guidelines to Authors and Typists" is available on request from the editor and should be obtained before the final typing of the manuscript.

Send all manuscripts and editorial correspondence to the editor: Robert N. Emde, Department of Psychiatry, University of Colorado School of Medicine, 4200 East Ninth Avenue, Box C268, Denver, Colorado 80262.

Child Development Research and Social Policy

Volume 1
Edited by Harold W. Stevenson and Alberta E. Siegel

To a child, family and school seem to be the shaping forces of life. But forces outside the family and school affect children's development and growth. Policymakers, teachers, and health professionals need the latest findings in child development research if they are to create programs that nurture children.

This volume, the first in a series commissioned by the Committee on Social Policy of the Society for Research in Child Development, highlights research on important contemporary social issues:

> **Luis M. Laosa**, Social Policies toward Children of Diverse Ethnic, Racial, and Language Groups in the United States
>
> **John A. Butler, Barbara Starfield**, and **Suzanne Stenmark**, Child Health Policy
>
> **Robert E. Emery, E. Mavis Hetherington**, and **Lisabeth Fisher**, Divorce, Children, and Social Policy
>
> **Samuel J. Meisels**, Prediction, Prevention, and Developmental Screening in the EPSDT Program
>
> **Stephen A. Richardson**, Deinstitutionalization and Institutionalization of Children with Mental Retardation
>
> **Jacquelynne S. Eccles** and **Lois W. Hoffman**, Sex Roles, Socialization, and Occupational Behavior
>
> **Ernesto Pollitt, Cutberto Garza**, and **Rudolph L. Leibel**, Nutrition and Public Policy
>
> **Judith Torney-Purta**, Political Socialization and Policy: The United States in a Cross-national Context

Anyone whose work influences the welfare of children

- educators
- government officials
- researchers
- pediatricians

- mental health professionals
- social workers
- legal professionals
- journalists

needs this volume

1984   LC: 84-50197   520 p.

Cloth $30 (ISBN: 0-226-77396-5)
Paper $15 (ISBN: 0-226-77397-3)

TO ORDER: Send check, purchase order, or complete charge card (Visa or MasterCard) information to The University of Chicago Press, Journals Division, P.O. Box 37005, Chicago, IL 60637.